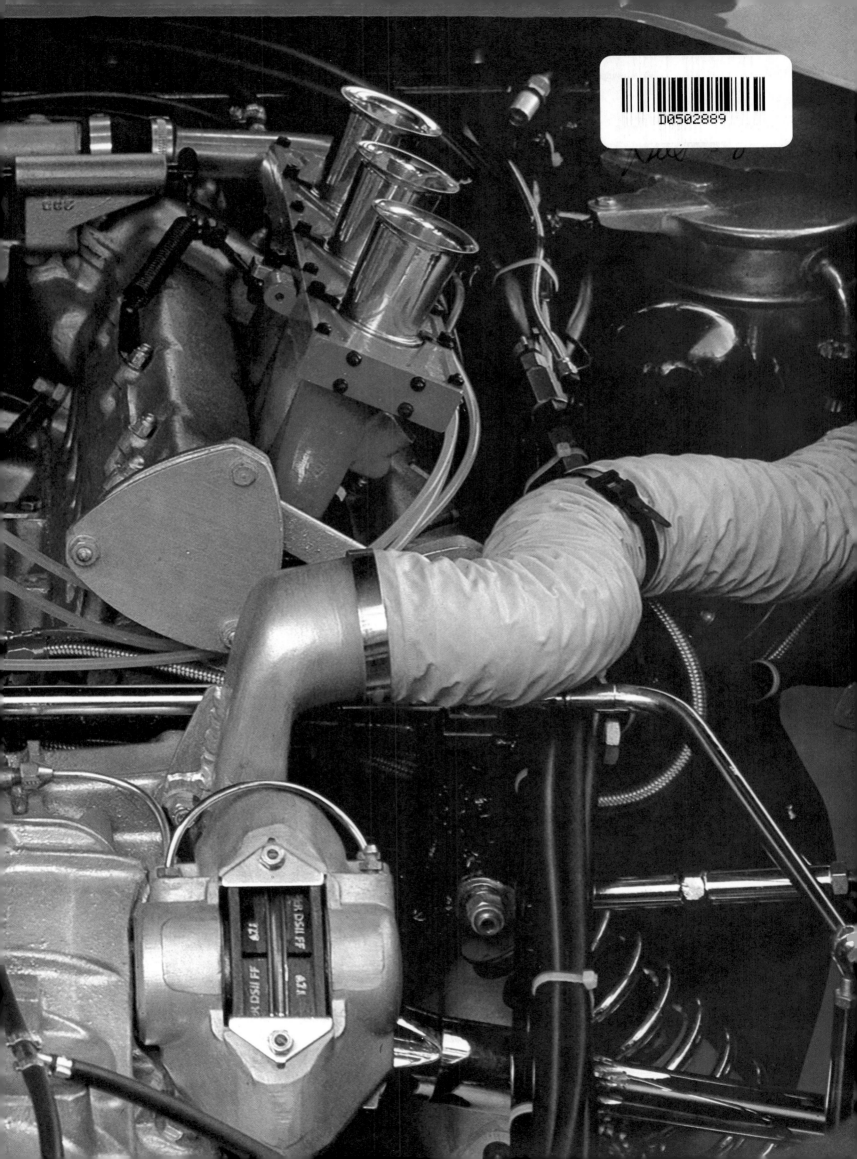

Great Marques
FERRARI

GREAT MARQUES
FERRARI

Godfrey Eaton

General Editor
John Blunsden
Foreword by
Jody Scheckter

octopus

Author's note

There are three people I would like to thank in particular for their assistance on this book; they are Geoff Willoughby, Dick Kitchingman and Victor Pigott as I consider them to have the best all round knowledge of the marque, the former on the gran turismo and sports racing cars and the latter two on the grand prix cars.

Thanks are also due to all those members of the Ferrari Owners' Club in the UK who very kindly allowed their cars to be photographed for inclusion in this volume. Where possible, owners of the cars, at the time of photography, are mentioned in the captions to the illustrations. The photographers told me they were shown every courtesy by members of the club whom they visited for photographic sessions and I cannot close without thanking them for the excellence of their photography.

Godfrey Eaton

ENDPAPERS, PAGES 1, 2/3, 4/5 *D. Mason-Styrron's superbly restored 206 SP. Only 15 were built and they were raced by the works in 1966 and 1967. With a V6 2-litre engine, it produces 250 bhp.*

PAGES 6/7 *Jody Scheckter, 1979 World Champion, in the Ferrari 312 T4 at the 1979 Spanish Grand Prix at Járama.*

First published in 1980 by Octopus Books Limited, 59 Grosvenor Street, London W1

©1980 Octopus Books Limited

ISBN 0 7064 1257 5

Produced by Mandarin Publishers Limited, 22a Westlands Road, Quarry Bay, Hong Kong

Printed in Hong Kong

PROVA ⯎ MO-53

Contents

Foreword by
Jody Scheckter

I can remember that at the age of 12 I knew I wanted to be a racing driver. I wanted to race cars. Any sort of cars, so long as they had four wheels. Names of marques didn't mean anything to me at that point.

I graduated through go-karts at 14 to 50 cc motorbikes and eventually to saloon cars on the tracks of South Africa. By the time I got to Europe in 1971 I knew that the sort of car I wanted to race was a single seater. Again no particular name or marque, just a single seater. It wasn't until I was into

Formula 2 racing that names began to have any real meaning for me; it was at this point that I began to be aware that Formula 1 was a distinct possibility for me.

I started off by thinking, like most young racers, that getting into any grand prix car would be something of an achievement. Then suddenly I began to think selectively for the first time. There were good teams and bad teams; there were ordinary teams and magic teams. It wasn't very long before I decided that Ferrari was the most 'magic' of all.

They had the reputation, the tradition and the long history of producing the most exciting of cars. And of course they had at the head of the operation the man who in his own lifetime had become a legend – Enzo Ferrari himself. They were the only racing team who actually did everything themselves. They built the car, the engine and the gearbox unlike the British 'kit car' teams. Don't take that as a knock at the users of

the British Standard Cosworth unit. It's not meant to be. It's just that you've got to have respect for an operation that designs and builds the whole thing from the floor upwards.

Ferrari, even for a hard-bitten grand prix driver, has a rather special charisma about it. I know that when I'm old and telling my grandchildren about my racing days I'll tell them that I drove for the Ferrari grand prix team and they'll know who I'm talking about. I won't have to explain who Ferrari was.

The people who work at Ferrari, both in the racing shop and in the factory, have a special sense of purpose about them. They give the impression of caring more about their job and their product than any other group of people I've met. Their devotion to their work and the cars they produce is almost a religion. Before I joined the team Enzo Ferrari said very little to me in terms of persuasion. One thing he did say very

simply was, join me and I will make you Champion of the World. I did, and he did. Winning it and working with the team was a tremendous pleasure and a great satisfaction.

I drive a Ferrari on the road (a bronze 400) not because it's part of the deal – I actually paid for it – but because I happen to like the cars and believe in them. This book tells some of the background and the magic that I have enjoyed being a small part of. Enjoy it. I did.

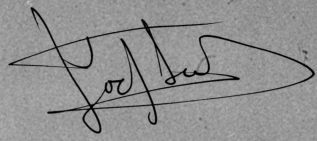

The aspirant

In the present world of mass communication the media create instant heroes for their readers and listeners to feed upon, and with equal promptness they may dismiss or destroy them. However, there are still a few living legends and among these is Enzo Ferrari and, although even in his native Italy the press has done its utmost at times to destroy the man who has presided over his 'empire' with an autocracy that went out of fashion many years ago, it has never succeeded.

Enzo Ferrari was born on 18 February 1898 on the outskirts of Modena but since his birth was not registered until two days later, in Italian law 20 February is the official date of his birth. His father owned a metal workshop adjoining the family house and was modestly prosperous, for how otherwise could he have afforded the luxury of a car during the early years of this century? In due course his father added a motor-repair shop to the business and Enzo learned the basic automobile skills here, though he was also offered the opportunity to study engineering at college. That he did not take this opportunity was a decision he regretted later, but he was wise enough in the years to come to pick the right man for any project he had in mind, and this flair was acknowledged by Alfa Romeo after he joined that company at Milan in 1920.

During Enzo's formative years his father would accompany him to watch races on the local circuits. Like all youths he had his heroes: his were Vincenzo Lancia and Felice Nazzaro. His ambition to become a racing driver was fired but World War I intervened. At the end of hostilities, during which he had a wretched time, he returned to the world of cars. Refused a job at Fiat, although he had a letter of introduction, his luck did not desert him for he found a position, as tester, in a specialist car business that modified Lancia light truck chassis, rebodying them and then selling them as passenger vehicles. However, on one of his frequent trips to Milan he met Ugo Sivocci, who was chief tester for Costruzioni Meccaniche Nazionali, another firm specializing in chassis and engine rebuilds from left-over parts, in this case from the Isotta Fraschini factory. As there was a chance to drive one of the cars in races he joined Sivocci and in 1919 managed a respectable fourth place in a CMN at the Parma–Reggio de Berceto hill climb, and during the same year he and Sivocci drove CMNs in the Targa Florio. Sivocci secured seventh place but Ferrari failed to finish in the allotted time as he had been delayed by a local political rally in one of the small townships on the race route.

By 1920 he had moved up in the world, joining Alfa Romeo as a works driver and taking one of the cars to second place in that year's Targa Florio. Sivocci had, in the meantime, come over to the Milanese firm; with Giuseppe Campari and Antonio Ascari the four men made a formidable driver combination and in the 1921 Targa Florio only Ascari failed to finish, with Campari third, Sivocci fourth and Ferrari fifth. Although Ferrari drove in a number of other races his effective career as a works driver ended around 1923 as Alfa Romeo considered that his administrative abilities far outweighed his prowess as a driver.

It was during his period as a driver that the prancing horse insignia came his way and was eventually used as the logo for his Scuderia (racing team) when it was formed. It is difficult to separate myth or legend from fact regarding his acquisition of the insignia, and though after nearly 60 years the truth may be immaterial, the matter is nonetheless of interest. The story goes that the Baracca family presented Enzo with a piece of fabric, from the fuselage of their son's Spad S13 aircraft, on which a prancing horse was displayed, after he had won a race on the del Savio circuit in 1923. In fact, the prancing horse, or *cavallino rampante*, was the insignia of Squadriglia 91a, which Francesco Baracca commanded, and the marking was perpetuated after World War 2 by 4a Aerobrigata, which flew F86E Sabres and F104G Fiat-built Starfighters. This being so it is difficult to believe the usual tale that the prancing horse was part of the Baracca family crest. The original prancing horse was a fiery-looking steed standing on both hind legs and with a drooping tail, and perhaps this was revamped later into the present insignia, a prancing horse standing on its nearside hind leg and with a rampant tail. The Pininfarina version suggests that, as Ferrari's brother served with and died in the same squadron as Baracca, the Countess Baracca indicated to Enzo that the insignia would be an appropriate memento to use as a logo on his cars. In any case the badge did not appear on any car until Ferrari formed his own racing team, Scuderia Ferrari, in December 1929.

This decision, which marked another phase in Enzo's life, meant leaving Alfa Romeo but the severance was amicable for the Milanese firm was quite happy to hand over and leave the racing of their cars to his Scuderia. In addition he was given the job of servicing customers' competition cars and also an area, as a concessionaire, to sell Alfa Romeo models. When he set up on his own he took with him a number of key personnel including his friend, Luigi Bazzi, a brilliant technical engineer. One individual who did not look on the new arrangement with any favour was Vittorio Jano, the chief designer for Alfa Romeo, a man Ferrari had enticed from Fiat some years before. While at Fiat Jano had not only designed that company's racing cars and other models but had also been team manager, and he felt that Alfa Romeo should have entrusted its racing team to his care and not to an outsider's

In 1932 came the advent of the famous Alfa Romeo Type B Monoposto (known universally as the P3) which showed its exhausts to all other entrants on the circuits. After one season, however, it was withdrawn and Ferrari was left with the Monza models, which were outdated and no longer competitive. This was indeed a blow to his morale and new-found prestige and while he still ran the cars he also turned his attention to motorcycle racing. In Italy his successes for two seasons with the radial four-valve Rudges earned the Scuderia the Italian championships for two years running in the 250, 350 and 500 cc classes—valuable publicity that kept his name to the forefront in racing. His two-wheel team consisted of at least ten Rudges and in addition a few 'cammy' Nortons.

By this time the might of the German government-sponsored Mercedes-Benz cars was being felt on the circuits—not to mention the Auto Unions—and, although the Alfa Romeos were updated and won an important race now and again, the factory, which had been taken over by the Italian government in 1932, did not have the finances to match the challenge with new cars. It was a low period for Italian racing and the Scuderia Ferrari, but the countenance of failure was never a trait in Enzo's make-up and so with Luigi Bazzi's connivance and with the assistance of Arnaldo Roselli, borrowed from Alfa Romeo, two Bimotores were built from Alfa parts. These monsters had an engine fore and aft of the cockpit and were identical apart from engine capacity; one had a total displacement of 6330 cc and other 5810 cc. These 'youthful follies', as Bazzi termed the cars, were for Formule Libre races and as a challenge to the German domination in racing. They were the fastest racing machines of the period, topping 320 km/h (200 mph), but no tyres had been manufactured to date (apart from those used for record breaking) that could withstand the power put down by their rear wheels on a long-distance race, so pit stops for tyre changing were frequent and, therefore, loss of time in races was the result. Both cars were extremely reliable and one was eventually sold to Austin Dobson, who raced it at Brooklands, and the other was broken up. These cars, being the brain children of Ferrari and Bazzi, can therefore be counted as the first Ferraris built even though constructed from Alfa parts.

In 1937, with little else to occupy his time, as the new Alfas were not really raceworthy against the German opposition, Ferrari had authority from the works to build a racing voiturette to compete against the many smaller-capacity cars for which classes were available in short- and long-distance events. Gioacchino Colombo was loaned by the Alfa factory and a new car was conceived, the Alfetta 158 with a 1.5-litre straight-8 engine. It was from this design that the Alfa Romeo 159 finally emerged to win four grand prix championship rounds against the three won by the 375 F1 Ferraris in 1951, before Alfa Romeo quit the racing scene until re-emerging in the Championship of Makes races about 20 years later.

Although 1929, when he formed his own racing team, was an important year for Ferrari an even more significant year was 1938, for that was when the Milanese firm decided to race its cars under its own banner, calling the team the Alfa Corse. Ferrari returned all the cars, equipment and other assets to the factory and was then invited to administer the racing department—but, having been in command of his own organization for so many years, he could hardly have been expected to settle down and work under someone else's management. Consequently it was not long before he fell out with Ugo Gobbato, the Alfa manager, over the overriding influence of a Spanish engineer, Wilfredo Ricart. Finally, this led Enzo to resign and back he went to Modena, taking with him Luigi Bazzi, Alberto Massimino and one or two others. Once more Ferrari was his own man, having severed for all time his 18-year connection with Alfa Romeo, but he had to wait until after World War 2 before the new era could begin.

Under the terms of the separation Ferrari was banned from building or racing any cars bearing his own name for a period of four years. While keeping strictly to the letter of these terms he did, however, construct two sports racing cars for the 1940 Mille Miglia and named them Vettura

PAGES 8/9 *Ferrari at the wheel of the ES Sport Alfa Romeo before the 1923 Targa Florio. He failed to finish and Sivocci won in a similar car.* RIGHT *A happy Enzo in the same car.* INSET *The smile of victory in later years.*

815 (the 8 standing for the number of cylinders and 15 for the engine capacity, i.e. 1.5 litres); they were built from Fiat parts.

In 1946 Ferrari was in business again and gathering around him a team capable of designing the type of car he admired above all, a car with 12 cylinders, such as the twin-6 Packard and the V12 Delage, and by 1947 a single overhead camshaft V12 appeared with a cubic capacity of 1500 cc and designated a 125. It was a sports-racing car and the first Formula 1 machine followed one year later.

Over a period of 32 years Ferrari has never been out of the grand prix arena and, unlike most constructors, the engines with which he has powered his cars have been 'home designed' and 'home built' and not bought off the shelf. At times he was not always successful—with designs behind the times, poor teamwork and even a complete walk-out of key men — but he has always had the resilience to come back, usually making a shattering impact. Never lost for a new idea, he has given his Formula 1 cars three different versions of V12 units; there have been two flat-12s; two V8s (one of which was the Lancia D50 designed by Vittorio Jano and handed over when that firm was in financial distress); three V6s; and two in-line 4s. All of these could be modified when the occasion or necessity demanded. Formula cars aside, there were the in-line 6s and a variety of experimental engines, from the in-line two-cylinder to the W18. There are many traps for the unwary, and even the knowledgeable, when attempting to research and write about the different designs.

Ferrari has used some three systems of designations, which the student needs to understand. However, he also appears to have proceeded by whimsy now and again, which can cause confusion in the minds of many people even though such designations might appear logical to the factory. The early racing cars and the current production models are designated by taking the capacity of one cylinder in cubic centimetres and multiplying it by the number of cylinders to give the total displacement, thus the 1.5-litre V12 Formula 1 was designated 125 F1.

A second method was used from 1957 whereby the total capacity and number of cylinders are indicated, for example the 246 F1 was a 2.4-litre V6, the 158 F1 a 1.5-litre V8, and the 312 series of F1 cars were 3-litre flat-12s. As already stated there are some inconsistencies, for the first flat-12 built in 1964/5 should by right be called a 1512 F1 (1.5-litre flat 12), whereas it was designated 512 F1; this might give the impression that the 512 M and S cars were similar but these in fact were the 5-litre V12 sports-racing machines used in the CanAm races and also for the sports-car championship series.

The third system was primarily for factory use and gave project numbers to engines based on the order of appearance of what were intended as racing cars: an example was project 116, which was the 2.5-litre in-line-2 and designated 252 F1. The odd ones were the Squalo and Supersqualo of the 1953–5 season and here speculation suggests that the 553 Squalo indicated a 1953 modification of the 500 series, and the 555 Supersqualo the final development of the engine in 1955. The Ferrari Lancia 801 (a development of the original Lancia D50) might suggest that it was an eight-cylinder F1 car—which of course it was—but the designation is not at all clear and has no place in the ordered nomenclature scheme.

What motivates a man such as Ferrari to continue in an increasingly expensive sport when for almost half of his 32 years as a constructor his Formula 1 cars have not been on top? No one can know but, like a number of other men, he must have a driving force that impels him to overcome adversity, even at times of personal loss, as when his son Dino died. Although the factory is better known for its main racing department, sight should not be lost of the great contribution he has made in the past to motor racing by supporting sports and GT racing. There are many who may have now forgotten the years of pre-eminence of such cars as the 250 V12 series and their immediate successors the P series; all these dominated the circuits whether in short- or long-distance events. Nor should the racing world forget other seasons of dominance, for example when the 500 F2 cars swept all opposition aside in 1952–3, winning 14 world championship races in a row.

Ferraris won the gruelling Targa Florio races in 1948, 1949, 1958, 1961, 1962, 1965 and 1972, and the Mille Miglia from 1948 to 1953 and again in 1956 and 1957. Almost every important race in the motor-sport calendar has been won by a Ferrari proving not only that they were and are fast cars but—just as important—reliable, for Ferrari has laid the greatest stress on the design and meticulous construction of his power plants.

It was Lord Nuffield, when plain Mr Morris, who made the somewhat rash statement in the early 1930s that racing does not improve the breed, for this has been disproved many times with cars as well as horses. There can be no argument that Ferrari's race-bred cars have improved his passenger vehicles down the years, culminating in the present range of the V8s, a V12 and a flat-12.

Ferrari is now in his 83rd year and those who have supported and continue to support the marque must wonder how much longer he can continue in the racing game. Also, the influence he still exerts on the Fiat management over the production side of GT cars is an unknown quantity: although he is supposed to have relinquished his executive position, it is difficult to believe that he has had only a minor say in their design as his touch is still evident. Also, he still makes a traditional appearance every year to announce to the press details of new vehicles, plus any modifications to the racing cars.

It can be said without fear of contradiction that over the years only two other makes have been invested with such aura and mystique by both the knowledgeable and the ordinary enthusiast. They are Bugatti and Alfa Romeo—and Enzo had more than a passing interest in the latter.

At the beginning of this chapter reference was made to the hostility of the Italian press to Enzo Ferrari for a number of reasons, none of which could be considered valid; it was in all probability his autocratic stance that upset them and, more than anything, the failure of his racing cars over many years in the Italian GP. But when a victory is forthcoming in the race every pressman, every adman climbs on the bandwagon.

On Sunday 9 September 1979 the Italian press had something to celebrate and Enzo was their god, for his red cars had won a notable one-two victory at Monza in the Italian GP when Jody Scheckter crossed the finishing line first, with Gilles Villeneuve second in hot pursuit, and to add to their joy—even though he was not Italian—Jody took the drivers' championship. (A lot of credit must also be given to the reliability of the cars and the efficiency of the Ferrari team which gave both drivers virtually a trouble-free season.) They had had to wait 13 years for such a victory for it was back in 1966 that the Italian, Lodovico Scarfiotti, and the Englishman, Michael Parkes, had scored a one-two win in the Italian GP.

Surely no victory could have been sweeter to a man who, in the twilight of his long life, could look back over 33 years and ponder the fact that he had designed and built what many consider to be the finest racing cars in the world and had also upheld the prestige of Italian automobile craftsmanship. Forza Ferrari!

John Surtees waits calmly in the 512 F1 flat-12 before being pushed to the front row of the grid for the 1965 Italian GP at Monza. A relaxed Enzo looks on while in the background Ferrari mechanics check Bandini's car.

The in-line 4s

The racing cars

After hostilities had ceased in 1945 it naturally took a while before motor racing could be resumed on any scale at grand prix level. Fuel shortages prevailed and only a limited number of rather tired prewar cars were still available, plus a few laid-up works vehicles such as the 1.5-litre supercharged Tipo 158 Alfa Romeo, assorted Maseratis, and the 4.5-litre Lago Talbot. All, however, required various degrees of restoration and modification to make them reliable and raceworthy.

In the wings there were several new constructors awaiting an opportunity to display their design talents, among them Enzo Ferrari, who had had a hand in designing the Alfa Romeo Bimotores and the Alfetta when he was still with the Milanese firm, and had built two in-line eight-cylinder Vettura 815s after he left.

The major races during that early postwar period consisted of mainly Formule Libre, Formula 1 and 2 and sports-racing events. With such a variety Ferrari decided his engines would have to serve at least two, if not three, purposes using a basic chassis. A highly tuned derivative would be used for formula racing and a less stressed engine for his sports-racing cars. Initially he had in mind the V12 configuration he admired and he invited Gioacchino Colombo to return to his team as chief designer

(Colombo had helped in the design of the 158 Alfetta in 1938). In 1946 he also engaged Aurelio Lampredi as junior to Colombo, but Lampredi became dissatisfied with his terms of employment, and went off to work for the Isotta Fraschini factory. Although Lampredi was not a trained automobile engineer Ferrari held him in such high regard that he felt that his loss might impede his own future plans and ambitions so he offered him a new contract to lure him back. Lampredi duly returned, and in the winter of 1950–1 Colombo went back to Maserati.

The 500 F2 and 625 F1

During 1950 Ferrari could see that the immediate future of motor racing would tend to lie with 2-litre unblown Formula 2 cars. Although he had V12s of this capacity in both blown and unblown form, they were being harassed on the circuits by four-cylinder cars that were less thirsty and therefore were not being delayed so long by pit stops for fuel.

Consequently, in 1951 Lampredi was given the job of producing 2- and 2.5-litre four-cylinder cars for the 1952–3 seasons. The 2-litre cars were intended for Formula 2 and the 2.5-litre engines were built in readiness for 1954, when new Formula 1 regulations were to come into force.

One of the main reasons for abandoning the V12 unblown cars in

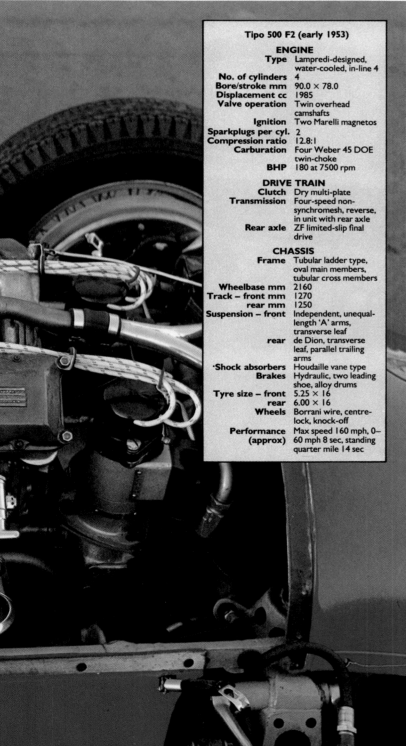

Tipo 500 F2 (early 1953)	
ENGINE	
Type	Lampredi-designed, water-cooled, in-line 4
No. of cylinders	4
Bore/stroke mm	90.0 × 78.0
Displacement cc	1985
Valve operation	Twin overhead camshafts
Ignition	Two Marelli magnetos
Sparkplugs per cyl.	2
Compression ratio	12.8:1
Carburation	Four Weber 45 DOE twin-choke
BHP	180 at 7500 rpm
DRIVE TRAIN	
Clutch	Dry multi-plate
Transmission	Four-speed non-synchromesh, reverse, in unit with rear axle
Rear axle	ZF limited-slip final drive
CHASSIS	
Frame	Tubular ladder type, oval main members, tubular cross members
Wheelbase mm	2160
Track – front mm	1270
rear mm	1250
Suspension – front	Independent, unequal-length 'A' arms, transverse leaf
rear	de Dion, transverse leaf, parallel trailing arms
Shock absorbers	Houdaille vane type
Brakes	Hydraulic, two leading shoe, alloy drums
Tyre size – front	5.25 × 16
rear	6.00 × 16
Wheels	Borrani wire, centre-lock, knock-off
Performance (approx)	Max speed 160 mph, 0–60 mph 8 sec, standing quarter mile 14 sec

favour of an in-line four-cylinder engine for Formula 2 racing was the fact that such a power plant would give more torque out of corners, and Ferrari anticipated around 100 bhp per litre.

The bore and stroke of the 2-litre engine was 'oversquare' (i.e. the bore was larger than the stroke) at 90 × 78 mm, and the 2.5-litre had a 94 × 90 mm bore and stroke. Ferrari decided to use the larger capacity unit as a test bed for the 2-litre chassis.

Since the Colombo and Lampredi engines formed the basis of most Ferrari power units it is appropriate that some details of their design should be given. Perhaps it should be stated at this stage that it was on the reliability of his engines that Enzo Ferrari laid the greatest stress, for an inspection of the chassis of those years shows them to have been invariably basic in design and at times crudely constructed. This led on a number of occasions to poor performances simply because it was not possible to deliver the full power to the rear driving wheels.

The following data on the Lampredi design refer specifically to the unblown 2.5-litre engine, although they also apply to the 2-litre unblown unit. Later we shall cover the V12s that preceded the in-line 4s.

The chassis (a scaled-down version of the V12 375 F1 design) was constructed with a steel oval frame 11 cm (4.4 in) deep and 5.5 cm (2.16 in) wide with a thickness of 1.5 mm (0.6 in). For rigidity the frame was cross-braced using large tubes at front and rear, with smaller tubes behind the engine and in front of the gearbox. The structure ahead of the cockpit was strengthened and to give added stiffness U-section longitudinal tubes were placed fore and aft. A welded upper structure was formed for the bodywork, which used aluminium panels.

A de Dion rear axle was employed, the tube passing behind the main drive casing with a groove providing transverse location for the universally jointed halfshafts and hubs. Transverse leaf springs were low mounted and two Houdaille vane-type shock absorbers provided the damping. The front suspension also had transverse leaf springs low mounted at the end of the frame and, on the early models, connected to the upper members of the unequal-length wishbones via an articulated rod (in later types the two main leaves were attached directly to the lower wishbones). Damping was by Houdaille vane-type shock absorbers on separate links with a kingpin between the links and the wishbones.

The jointed steering column was on the left and connected, through three universal joints, to a worm-and-wheel steering box. The cross steering linkage had a sleeve arm with two short track rods mounted in front of the wheel centres. Light alloy drums with two leading shoes were used for both front and rear hydraulic brakes. It is interesting to note that to get the greatest diameter possible for the brakes, including deep fins for cooling, there was a marked offset from wheel centre and projection of the kingpin. Drums were 35 cm (13.8 in) in diameter with a friction area of 1580 cm^2 (245 sq in): either 15 in or more usually 16 in centre-lock Borrani wire wheels were fitted with Englebert or Pirelli tyres (5.25/16 or 5.50/16 at the front and 6.50/16 or 7.00/16 at the rear were typical sizes).

Except for the normal Ferrari practice of not using head gaskets, the engine departed in most respects from the former principles employed

PAGES 14/15 AND THIS PAGE This is believed to be Alberto Ascari's 1953 British GP-winning car. The four-cylinder 2-litre 500 F2 won 30 out of 33 championship races in two years. Now in the Donington Collection.

by Colombo. Five Vandervell 'Thinwall' main bearings supported the crankshaft in a deep aluminium-alloy crankcase/cylinder block. Water and oil pumps were driven, at the bottom, by a train of gears from the nose of the crankshaft. A second train drove the twin overhead camshafts, which operated two valves per cylinder at an included angle of 58 degrees. The valves were closed by hairpin springs and the light-alloy tappets, fitted between the valves and camshafts, were controlled by double coil springs. Twin magnetos were driven from the rear of the camshafts; in later models they were located at the front and driven by the crankshaft.

Four steel liners were screwed into the combustion-chamber recesses with the cylinder head cast integrally with the waterjackets, making sound gas and water seals. Two rubber O-rings provided oil and water seals, being located by a flange at the base.

The 80/20 petrol/alcohol mixture of fuel was fed by two twin-throat Weber 50 DCO carburettors, but in later models the 50 DCOA carburettor was used. Fuel consumption was said to be 4.25 km per litre (12 mpg). A carefully thought-out exhaust system led the gases from cylinders 1 and 4 into a single pipe, from cylinders 2 and 3 into another pipe, the two pipes then combining into one larger-diameter pipe. Early 2-litre cars had four stub exhaust pipes and four single-throat 45 DOE

carburettors, but both these features were later discarded, and the layout then followed the pattern of the 2.5-litre unit.

With such a large combustion-chamber area, cooling was of prime importance. The water pump impelled the coolant into a passage within the main bearing housing and thence to the cylinder head, where it was drawn off by four pipes bolted to cored passages running between the twin sparkplug seating but offset to the inlet side.

Both the 2- and 2.5-litre engines were noted for their reliability, with the peak of the torque curve being reached at slightly under 5000 rpm. Power was transmitted to the non-synchromesh four-speed-and-reverse gearbox through a dry multi-plate clutch, the gearbox being mounted at the rear. The compression ratio of the early 2-litre car (1951) was 11.5:1, but by late 1953 it had been raised to 13:1. For the 2.5-litre car it was 11.0:1 in 1951–3, increased to 12.8:1 by mid-1954. The early 2.5-litre engine (1951–3) had a power output of around 210 bhp at 7000 rpm, which was increased by 1954 to 260 bhp at 7500 rpm. The first 2-litre units developed 165 bhp at 7000 rpm, increased to 185 bhp at 7500 rpm with the late 1953 engines.

Modifications of a minor order were made from year to year. The cockpit was neat and simple with the minimum of instrumentation. In 1951

the 2-litre car weighed 560 kg (1100 lb) but by late 1953 this had increased to 615 kg (1356 lb); the 2.5-litre car remained 600 kg (1323 lb).

The 2.5-litre car, known as the 625, and built to the 1954 Formula I regulations, made its first appearance at the 1951 GP at Bari, where it was driven by Piero Taruffi into a respectable third place. Although this car was used in practice later that year before the Italian GP at Monza it was a non-starter there, being returned to the factory before the race. Before the 1951 season ended two cars, using the 2-litre unit and designated 500 F2, were raced at the Modena GP by Luigi Villoresi and Alberto Ascari. Both cars proved superior to the V12 loaned to Froilan Gonzalez, and although Villoresi did not finish the race, this debut augured well for the 1952 season when Formula 2 racing was to supplant Formula I. (As Alfa Romeo had pulled out of racing after beating the Ferraris at the Spanish GP, the Modena concern was left with no opposition in the 'premier division', hence the temporary abandonment of Formula I.)

The years 1952 and 1953 were certainly Ferrari's for the 500 F2 was the most successful grand prix car ever raced, winning 14 world

Maurice Trintignant driving a 2.5-litre 625 F1 took the chequered flag 20 sec ahead of Eugenio Castellotti (Lancia D50) to win the 1955 Monaco GP.

championship events in a row during that period. The remarkably successful works cars were beaten only three times in 33 races, at Rheims in 1952 by Gordini (Jean Behra) and at Syracuse and Monza in 1953 by Maserati (Baron Emanuel de Graffenried and Juan Manuel Fangio). Ascari, Scuderia Ferrari's number one driver, took the driver's world championship in both years.

The success of these two years should have continued in 1954, for the 625 F1 had proved its reliability and the works drivers liked its handling characteristics. However, the highly organized and financed Mercedes-Benz team had re-entered the fray with some exciting cars which were to prove both fast and reliable while the Maseratis were also quick but unreliable. In fact 1954 was to be another year of experimentation and it demonstrated once more the ability of the leading designers and engineers to produce, almost overnight, a new engine or even a chassis.

To overcome the lack of power the factory retained the lower half of the engine but used the reworked head of the 553 F1 Squalo (this type had made its debut in the spring of 1954). This did not prove wholly satisfactory. As an alternative the new engine was used in the 625 F1 chassis until the more potent version of this unit, the 555 F1 Supersqualo, giving 250 bhp at 7500 rpm, was installed. The overall performance,

Gonzalez wins heat 1 of the Daily
Express Trophy, Silverstone,
May 1954, in a 553 Squalo but
raced a 625 F1 in heat 2 as the 553
engine had seized. INSET Four-
cylinder 2.5-litre 553 engine shows
two twin-choke Weber carburettors and twin Marelli magnetos.

however, was not enhanced: there was no doubt the engine required more modification and testing. A further development of the 625 F1 chassis came in 1955 when the 750 Formule Libre engine made its debut with a bore of 100 mm and stroke of 90 mm for a displacement of 2999.6 cc. This unit, with an output of 290 bhp at 7500 rpm, was to power the 750 Monza.

The 553 F2, the 553 F1 and 555 F1, 1953–6

The original design of the 553 F2 appeared at Monza in 1953 as a Formula 2 car with an engine bore and stroke of 93 × 73.5 mm giving a displacement of 1997.2 cc. By the spring of 1954 the cylinders had been bored out to 100 × 79.5 mm with a total capacity of 2497 cc and the car, which used a multi-tubular spaceframe, was designated 553 F1.

In general terms the suspension followed that of the 625 F1 but the de Dion tube was now placed in front of the final-drive casing. The weight had been reduced by 10 kg (22 lb) and the centre of gravity lowered. The main feature was the placing of the fuel tanks at the sides of the body, resulting in a rather bulbous shape, hence the car's name Squalo ('Shark'). If its squat, aggressive appearance could have been translated into an equivalent performance on the track, the type should have carried on the

Tipo 860 Monza (1956)	
ENGINE	
Type	Lampredi designed, water-cooled, in-line 4
No. of cylinders	4
Bore/stroke mm	102.0 × 105.0
Displacement cc	3431.9
Valve operation	Twin overhead camshafts
Ignition	Two Marelli magnetos
Sparkplugs per cyl.	1
Compression ratio	8.5:1
Carburation	Two Weber 58 DCO/A3 twin-choke, sidedraft
BHP	280 at 6200 rpm
DRIVE TRAIN	
Clutch	Double dry plate
Transmission	Five-speed non-synchromesh, reverse, in unit with rear axle
Rear axle	de Dion
CHASSIS	
Frame	Large diameter welded tubular frame
Wheelbase mm	2350
Track – front mm	1308
rear mm	1280
Suspension – front	Independent, unequal-length 'A' arms, coil springs
rear	de Dion axle beam, transverse leaf, parallel trailing arms
Shock absorbers	Houdaille hydraulic, lever action
Brakes	Hydraulic, aluminium drums, iron liners
Tyre size – front	6.00 × 16
rear	7.00 × 16
Wheels	Borrani wire, centre-lock, knock-off
Performance (approx)	Max speed 150 mph, 0–60 mph 7 sec, standing quarter mile 14 sec

The 1954 860 Monza.
Owned by Wolf Zeuner.

good work of the 500 F2. Alas, there was little aggression and its handling characteristics were in keeping with its track record. As a result the works drivers preferred the older 625 F1.

The included angle of the valves had been increased to 100 degrees, which gave the engine the appearance of having a V cylinder configuration. The unit produced 240 bhp at 7500 rpm with a compression ratio 12.0:1 and was fed by two Weber 52 DCOA carburettors. It made its debut at Syracuse in 1954.

A further 10 bhp had been found by the end of the season and in an attempt to improve the handling the track was extended by 8 mm to 1278 mm (4 ft 2 in). During the winter the engine was worked on and by early 1955 the compression ratio had been raised to 14:1 and the output to 270 bhp/7500 rpm. It was now dubbed Supersqualo but in fact showed little improvement. By the late season a five-speed-and-reverse gearbox replaced the four-speed box and was mounted at the rear in unit with the ZF limited-slip final drive.

The final version of the Supersqualo in 1956 was powered by the Lancia D50 90-degree V8 unit.

The sports cars

It had been Ferrari practice from the early days to switch engines from grand prix to sports cars and the habit persisted with the in-line 4s. There were a number of obvious advantages to the system, not least that of being able to produce sports cars for customers. The first four-cylinder engine for sports-car racing was the 2.5-litre Lampredi grand prix unit, which was installed in either a 166 or 250 MM chassis. Together with a 3-litre four, the car was first seen at Monza in 1953.

During the winter of 1953–4 work went ahead on a new four-cylinder car based on the Tipo 555. This was to be the 750 Monza and followed the normal Lampredi practice. The two valves per cylinder were at an included angle of 85 degrees and for lightness the camshafts, while large in diameter, were bored throughout their length. Pistons were domed with indents for valve clearance and had two compression rings and two oil rings, one of them located below the wrist pin. There was dry-sump lubrication with pressure and scavenge pump in the front together with the gear train driving the camshafts. Two magnetos, later replaced by two distributors, sparked two plugs per cylinder. Also the early four-speed-

plus-reverse gearbox gave way to a five-speed box, both being rear mounted. In 1955 the single front-mounted leaf spring was replaced by coil springs.

At the Tourist Trophy in September 1955 a larger-capacity Monza appeared that had a bore and stroke of 102 × 105 mm for a displacement of 3431 cc. It will be noted that the stroke was greater than the bore (the first time for a Ferrari type). This was designated the 860 Monza and had limited successes.

With possible customers in mind Ferrari introduced the 500 Mondial using the 1952–3 F2 unit. In many respects the chassis followed the usual practice, as did the suspension. The model had strong opposition from the sports Maserati and to increase the power the cylinder head of the 553 F2 was substituted, and with the larger 45 DCO/A3 carburettors it developed 170 bhp at 7000 rpm. A few other modifications were carried out but these made little difference in practice, so Ferrari turned his attention to a new 2-litre four-cylinder engine conceived by Vittorio Jano and other members of the design team (Lampredi departed in 1955 and went to Fiat). The unit was to power the 500 Testa Rossa, which, making a

TOP AND ABOVE *500 Mondial was a successful sports racing car during 1954 and 1955 but had stiff opposition from Maserati. Owned by the Harrisons.*

first showing at the 1000 km Supercortemaggiore race at Monza on 24 June 1956, finished first, second, and fourth. The car appeared next at Le Mans, using the 625 F1 engine and designated 625 LM. It finished third overall.

A new 500 TRC was announced by Ferrari at his annual press day late in 1956. The car was for customers and not works use. The engine had the same dimensions as the Mondial, bore and stroke 90 × 78 mm, and used a head similar to the early 500 F2. A number of modifications were carried out including a strengthened crankshaft and rods, and the transmission was now engine-mounted with a live rear axle. Suspension was independent as usual but with coils all round. This was the last four-cylinder model, except for the delightful small ASA, nicknamed the Ferrarina. Conceived in 1957, the first model used to accompany the racing team all over Europe in the late 1950s and early 1960s. The design was finally sold off to the de Nora chemical company.

The in-line 6s and V6s

The 118 LM and 121 LM

Production of the in-line 6s was confined to two models, the 118 LM and the 121 LM, although there were variations such as the 446 Indianapolis car which used a Kurtis Kraft chassis. This latter car had been commissioned by 'Nino' Farina in 1955 but failed to qualify for the '500' race in 1956 and the following year was wrecked when it hit a wall with fatal results to its American driver.

The 118 LM was developed from the 2.5-litre 625 four-cylinder unit by adding two more cylinders, giving a displacement of 3747 cc. With the addition of two cylinders to the 3-litre Monza four engine the 121 LM had a capacity of 4412.5 cc. Similar in many respects to the Mondial engine, the 118 LM had screwed-in cylinder liners and twin overhead camshafts and produced 280 bhp at 6400 rpm. Three Weber 45 DCOA/3 carburettors were used and the two plugs per cylinder were fired through two Marelli distributors. Its first event was the 1000 km at Buenos Aires in January 1955 where Froilan Gonzalez was disqualified but the car had shown its potential by being in contention throughout the race. The only European success was achieved in the Tour of Sicily when driven by Piero Taruffi, and its last serious race was the 1955 Mille Miglia when four were entered: Umberto Maglioli managed third place and another car came in sixth. Also entered in the Mille Miglia was the Eugenio Castellotti 121 LM which led to the first control at Ravenna at an average of 191.5 km/h (119 mph); it was then retired, one of the reasons given being that it needed a complete tyre change. Three of this Tipo were sent to Le Mans but after four hours' or so racing all were eliminated. At the Swedish GP for sports cars Castellotti finished third behind Juan Manuel Fangio and Stirling Moss driving Mercedes 300 SLRs and while Castellotti was undoubtedly fastest, the rough surface of the track did not allow full power to be applied. After this race all three cars were sold to the United States.

Like the Mondial and Monza, the 118 and 121 LMs had welded tube frames using large-section longitudinal and cross members with smaller tubes for the various components and other attachments. Front suspension was independent with coils and unequal-'A' arms (wishbones) and a transverse leaf spring with de Dion tube was provided at the rear. A five-speed gearbox was in unit with the ZF limited-slip differential. The track of all four models was 1278 mm (4 ft 2 in) at the front and 1284 mm (4 ft 2½ in) at the rear but the wheelbases differed.

As happened now and again Ferrari lost interest in the in-line 6s although it did seem that the potential of the 121 LM could have been developed further. Instead the 860 Monza was to lead the sports-racing attack in 1956.

26

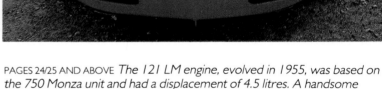

PAGES 24/25 AND ABOVE *The 121 LM engine, evolved in 1955, was based on the 750 Monza unit and had a displacement of 4.5 litres. A handsome sports-racing car, it was not very competitive. Owned by M. Spitzley.*

The front-engined 156 F2, 246 F1, 256 F1 and 296 M1

Attention must now be turned to the front-engined Dino V6, F2 and F1 cars. This name was given to all V6s after Enzo's son Alfredo, who was known as Dino, because it was he who suggested this configuration.

The first car in the series was the 156 F2 designed by Vittorio Jano and it followed, in many respects, his original Lancia D50 layout. Apart from the F2 car of 1957 there were seven variants of the 246 F1 and two 256 F1s in the series between 1957 and 1960, with capacities from 1860 cc to 2474.6 cc and bhp ratings from 215 at 8500 rpm to 295 at 8500 rpm. The earliest car (1957) had a bore and stroke of 78.6 × 64.5 mm and over the three-year period this increased to 86 × 71 mm.

The F2 chassis was a multi-tubular spaceframe with large-diameter main longitudinal members and the power units of the F1 cars used this frame up to early 1958 and again in 1960. Between mid-1958 and late 1959, although the spaceframe was used, it had smaller-diameter longitudinal members.

The F2 car can be taken as the basis for all the 246 F1 types and the modifications can be noted where they occur.

Suspension at the front used unequal-length 'A' arms, coil springs and anti-roll bar, and at the rear the well-tried transverse leaf spring was in evidence with a de Dion tube in a guide aft of the final drive casing. Universal-jointed halfshafts and double parallel radius rods completed the system. All-round, vane-type Houdaille shock absorbers were fitted as well as hydraulic drum brakes, while 16 in Borrani centre-lock wheels shod with Englebert tyres (5.50/16 front and 6.50/16 rear) were used. The wheelbase was 2160 mm (7 ft 1 in), front track 1270 mm (4 ft 2 in) and rear track 1240 mm (4 ft 1 in). A 65 degree V6 engine was mounted diagonally with the drive shaft to the left of driver. The bore and stroke was 70 × 64.5 mm to give a displacement of 1489.4 cc. The cylinder blocks, with cast-iron liners, were aluminium alloy, as was the crankcase, and three 38 DCN Weber carburettors fed fuel. Twin overhead camshafts to each cylinder bank were operated by chain and the two magnetos were driven from the front of the camshaft intakes. With two plugs per cylinder and a compression ratio at 10:1 the output was 175 bhp at 9000 rpm. Transmission was via a dry multi-plate clutch with four-speed-and-reverse box set transversely at the rear in unit with the usual ZF limited-slip final drive.

Tipo 246 F1 (mid-1958)

	ENGINE			CHASSIS	
Type	Jano-designed, water-cooled, 65-degree V6		Frame	Multi-tubular spaceframe with small-diameter members	
No. of cylinders	6		Wheelbase mm	2160	
Bore/stroke mm	85.0 × 71.0		Track – front mm	1240	
Displacement cc	2417		rear mm	1240	
Valve operation	Twin overhead camshafts per bank of cyls		Suspension – front	Unequal-length 'A' arms, coil springs, anti-roll bar	
Ignition	Two magnetos		rear	de Dion, transverse leaf spring, parallel radius rods	
Sparkplugs per cyl.	2				
Compression ratio	9.8:1		Shock absorbers	Front telescopic, rear Houdaille	
Carburation	Three Weber 42 DCN twin-choke, downdraft		Brakes	Hydraulic with cast-iron turbo finned drums	
BHP	275 at 8300 rpm		Tyre size – front	5.50 × 16	
	DRIVE TRAIN		rear	6.50 × 16	
Clutch	Dry multi-plate		Wheels	Borrani wire, centre-lock, knock-off	
Transmission	Four-speed-and-reverse gearbox mounted to right side of differential assembly		Performance (approx)	Max speed 170 mph, 0–60 mph 7 sec, standing quarter mile 12 sec	
Rear axle	ZF-limited slip and universally jointed halfshafts				

Phil Hill in the rear-engined 156 F1 was second in the 1961 Dutch GP. Von Trips, in a similar car, won.

INSET *Mike Hawthorn taking a 246 F1 to fifth place in the Dutch GP (Zandvoort, May 1958). The points helped him to become World Champion.*

The earliest Formula 1 car (1957) followed the pattern of the F2 but with an increase in bore to 78.6 mm (the displacement was now 1860 cc), and two magnetos driven from the rear of the camshaft intakes. Later in the year the capacity was 2195 cc with bore and stroke of 81 × 71 mm, and Weber 42 DCN carburettors replaced the 38s. For 1958 the displacement was up by 222.3 cc as the bore had been enlarged to 85 mm and during this period the power had risen from 270 bhp at 8300 rpm to 285 bhp at 8500 rpm. Also from mid-1958 telescopic shock absorbers replaced the Houdailles and the brakes had cast-iron turbo-finned drums, but these were to give way to Dunlop discs by the end of the season. Front and rear tracks were now the same at 1240 mm (4 ft 1 in). Further modifications were made for 1959; a five-speed-and-reverse gearbox was installed and the rear suspension used coil springs with Koni dampers, and the wheelbase was increased to 2220 mm (7 ft 3½ in).

Late 1958 brought the introduction of the 256 F1, which followed the pattern of the mid-1958 246 F1 but with the bore increased to 85 mm and stroke lengthened by 1 mm to give a capacity of 2451 cc with the bhp rising to 290. A minor modification to the engine was seen in the 1959 car with the displacement now 2474.6 cc and output 295 bhp at 8500 rpm. The four-speed-and-reverse box was replaced by five speeds and suspension modified to the 246 F1 1959 specification.

During the winter of 1959–60 the drive from the diagonally mounted engine was reversed and placed to the right of the driver's seat. The F2 chassis-frame design was in evidence with the main fuel tanks added to the sides and a small tank in the tail. A redesigned rear suspension used unequal-length 'A' arms, coil springs and, for damping, Koni shock absorbers were fitted. The track had been stretched by an additional 60 mm.

The front-engined Dinos had a chequered racing history, doing well on some occasions but being outclassed on others. However, the F1 and F2 cars could be considered successful since Mike Hawthorn took the 1958 world drivers' championship by one point from Moss but the British-built Vanwalls gave the Dinos a tough season, finally taking the manufacturers' award. Sadly, this season was marred by the death of Peter Collins; he crashed at the German GP and the works lost a fine sporting driver.

'Small is beautiful' could certainly be said of the 1958 front-engined Dinos. Aesthetically they could not be faulted with smooth lines and even the central bonnet fairing (at times a plastic hood) to accommodate the carburettors, appeared purposeful. The tail design of these handsome cars was just right and bore more than a resemblance to the rear end of the Lancia D50s.

Before leaving the formula Dinos, mention should be made of the 296 M1 of mid-1958, built specially for the Monza 500-mile event when European cars were in contention with the USAC Indianapolis racers. Speed was the essential factor with cars of up to 4.2 litres permitted on the banked section of the circuit. The 296 M1 was supported by two V12 Ferrari specials and, driven in the first heat by the American Phil Hill, was retired with magneto problems.

With a bore and stroke of 85 × 87 mm the 296 M1 displaced 2962.1 cc. Fuel was fed by three Weber 46 DCN carburettors. The power output was given as 310 bhp at 8000 rpm. The front suspension had telescopic shock absorbers and coil springs, at the rear coil springs with Konis were used and, with the anticipated high speeds on a far from smooth surface, additional Houdaille vane-type shock absorbers were fitted all round to give further essential damping. The wheels, 16 in front and 17 in rear, were centre-lock Borranis fitted with Firestone tyres.

Apart from the foregoing modifications the design was basically similar to the mid-1958 246 F1 cars. It did, however, have a wider body and the wheelbase was extended by 60 mm. This one-off appeared at the Nürburgring but with a 2417 cc engine (246 F1) and after a number of further modifications. It was used in practice by Hawthorn but did not race in the German GP.

The following year, 1959, was also an indifferent one for the Dinos which, apart from suspension and other modifications, included new bodywork by Medardo Fantuzzi. This was longer and wider with the exhausts carried low, not so handsome as the earlier cars but more purposeful and aggressive-looking. No world championships were gained in the season but the British driver, Tony Brooks, came third in the drivers' championship, winning the French and German GPs.

The 1962 196 SP belongs to a special prototype racing and sports car group. The rear-mounted V6 2-litre unit has been described as a 'jewel of a power plant'. This example has been restored meticulously by John Godfrey. A versatile car, it contested long-distance events and hill climbs.

Tipo 196 SP Dino (1962)

ENGINE		CHASSIS	
Type	Colombo-based, water-cooled, 60-degree V6 (rear mounted)	Frame	Welded multi-tubular steel
No. of cylinders	6	Wheelbase mm	2320
Bore/stroke mm	77.0 × 71.0	Track – front mm	1310
Displacement cc	1983	rear mm	1300
Valve operation	Single overhead camshaft per bank of cyls	Suspension – front	Independent, unequal-length 'A' arms, coil springs
Ignition	One Marelli distributor	rear	Independent, unequal-length 'A' arms, coil springs, parallel trailing arms
Sparkplugs per cyl.	1		
Compression ratio	9.8:1	Shock absorbers	Koni
Carburation	Three Weber 42 DCN twin-choke, downdraft	Brakes	Disc
		Tyre size – front	5.25 × 15
BHP	210 at 7500 rpm	rear	6.50 × 15
		Wheels	Borrani wire, centre-lock, knock-off
DRIVE TRAIN		Performance	Max speed 140 mph, 0–60 mph 7 sec, standing quarter mile 13 sec
Clutch	Multiple disc	(approx)	
Transmission	Five-speed non-synchromesh, reverse, direct drive in 5th		
Rear axle	Live		

The rear-engined 246 F1, 156 F2 and 156 F1

For Ferrari, 1960 was a year of transition as he had now taken up the idea of rear-mounted engines and both these and front-engined Dinos were entered in races. The rear-engined cars used both 2.5- and 1.5-litre units: the regulations were to change for 1961, allowing a maximum displacement of 1500 cc which was to remain in force until the end of 1965.

The first prototype rear-engined car was seen at Monaco in 1960, a 2.4-litre V6 using many of the 246 F1 parts and going under the same name. However, the dry multi-plate clutch was mounted at the rear of the five-speed gearbox, this being placed behind the engine and in unit with the final drive, and the brakes were mounted inboard. It was not a success and retired with final-drive trouble.

During July 1960 a much-revised 1957 1.5-litre V6 Dino 156 F2 appeared at the Solitude Ring in West Germany. The engine was rear-mounted with a bore and stroke of 73 × 59.1 mm and an output of 180 bhp. The car not only set a new lap record but won by a small margin of three seconds from a Porsche.

Ferrari was ready for the new formula in 1961 with two versions of the V6 Dino: the 65-degree unit and a redesigned 120-degree 156 F1 engine and new chassis. With the bore remaining at 73 mm the stroke was shortened to 58.8 mm giving a displacement of 1476.6 cc. Fuel was fed via two Weber 40 1F3C three-choke carburettors and output was 190 bhp at 9500 rpm. Both the 65- and 120-degree-engined cars had revised front ends with two intake nostrils.

The season of 1961 was highly successful for Ferrari with Phil Hill winning the world drivers' championship and the works taking the manufacturers' title. Hill, driving the 156 F1, won the Belgian and Italian Grands Prix and was runner up in the British.

Little was accomplished over the winter months since a wholesale walkout by the key staff took place and the racing department had to be built up anew. Gone was the familiar twin-nostril front and this omission was virtually the only feature to differentiate the cars of 1962 from the winners of the previous year. However, they were slower and their handling left much to be desired: all in all a miserable year.

New cars, a reorganized racing set-up and a new number one works driver, John Surtees, heralded 1963. The Dino 156 F1 still used the tubular spaceframe but the suspension was altered with the coil springs and shock absorbers mounted lower and at a greater angle. At the rear the 'A' arms were reversed and lowered with single upper links and longer radius rods. The 1.5-litre engine was now Bosch fuel-injected and produced 200 bhp

at 10,200 rpm. The wheelbase was extended to 2880 mm (7ft 10 in) and the wheels were now cast in magnesium. The car showed some form in the early events of the season and won at the Nürburgring.

For the Monza race it had been hoped to use the new Aero V8 car (this had an aircraft-type semi-monocoque form) but as the engine was not ready the Dino 156 F1 unit was installed. Surtees had to retire with a broken valve and damaged piston.

The works took the manufacturers' title in 1964 using the new chassis with both V6 and V8 engines, and John Surtees the drivers' world championship. Surtees' second place in the Mexican GP secured the title by a single point from Graham Hill. For 1980 Ferrari plans to return again to V6s for F1 racing with a new 1500 cc 120-degree turbo unit (designated 156 F1) which will share a revised chassis with the 3000 cc boxer engine. This car will be used on the faster circuits.

The 246 Tasman cars and 166 F2 V6 Dinos

By taking a 158 F1 chassis and installing a Dino 246 engine that gave 280 bhp, Ferrari felt he had produced a potent machine for the 1966 Tasman championship series in Australia and New Zealand. Unfortunately Surtees had been badly injured the previous September at a sports-car race meeting in Canada and the project was abandoned. The car was, however, used during the European season.

For Formula 2 cars the governing authority decreed that in future production engines should be used and Ferrari, therefore, designed a 2-litre V6 for sports-car racing and a 1.6-litre V6 for F2, and Fiat built the units; the latter engine was designated 166 F2. It was equipped with Lucas fuel injection and had 18 valves (2 intake and 1 exhaust per cylinder) with Marelli transistor ignition. The new chassis of semi-monocoque design and suspension followed the previous F1 layout. There were three versions of the engine, two of which had 24 valves (2 intakes, 2 exhausts per cylinder). The 166 F2 was a hard-worked car and competed in no fewer than 16 events during 1968, winning two European and three South American races towards the end of the season. A second attempt at the Tasman series was made in 1968 when Chris Amon campaigned a 166 F2 chassis with an 18-valve twin-ignition 246 engine and won two of the eight races and was well placed in four other events. Derek Bell joined Amon for the 1969 seven-event series using cars similar to the previous year. Amon won four events and was placed third in two; Bell had two seconds, a fourth, and two fifths. Both cars had nose spoilers and wings mounted over the engines; one of them was sold to New Zealander Graeme Lawrence who won the Tasman title in 1970.

The V6 SP cars

At his press conference in early 1961 Enzo Ferrari showed the 246 SP with a 2.4-litre 60-degree V6 double overhead camshaft engine; the original design of this unit went back to 1956. With a bore and stroke of 85 × 71 mm it displaced 2417 cc and had a compression ratio of 9.8:1. There were three double-choke 42 DCN Weber carburetters located in the 'V' of the engine and the power output at 8000 rpm was 270 bhp. The type's racing baptism was in the United States at the 1961 Sebring 12-hour race, in the hands of Wolfgang von Trips, where its phenomenal speed took it to first place before the steering arm broke.

Two of the cars contested the Targa Florio in Sicily without doubt the toughest race in the calendar, but the Phil Hill/Richie Ginther car was eliminated early on, and von Trips with Olivier Gendebien had a race-long struggle against the 2-litre Porsche of Stirling Moss and Jo Bonnier. The lap record fell with almost monotonous regularity, and on the last lap the Porsche, with a slender lead, succumbed to transmission failure to let von Trips take the chequered flag.

Rain getting into the 'works' via the louvres caused a minor setback to the two cars at the Nürburgring 1000 km race, although von Trips managed third place. A further miscalculation occurred during the Le Mans 24-hour race when von Trips ran out of fuel at Mulsanne when lying second after 16 hours of racing. However, the back-up team of Testa Rossas made it a one-two result with a 250 GT claiming third place.

The 246 SP cars proved that when Enzo Ferrari was convinced of the correctness of any decision, however late, he had the ability to make up time on the other constructors, for with the help of these rear-engined

THIS PAGE AND FOLLOWING TWO PAGES *Fifteen of these handsome 206 SPs were built. The 65-degree V6 2-litre unit with three valves per cylinder and fuel induction produced 240 bhp. Raced by the works in 1966 and 1967 in long-distance and hill climbs it had its successes. Also competed extensively in the UK. Restored by owner D. Mason-Sturror.*

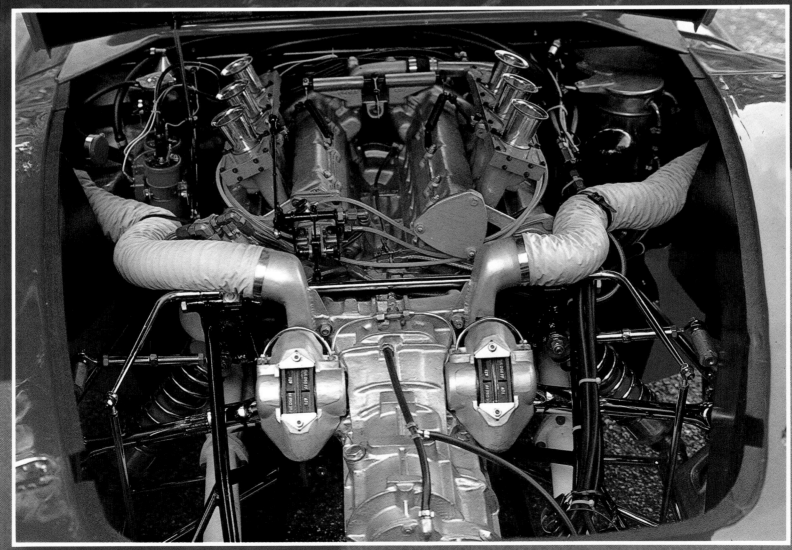

sports cars the factory won the manufacturers' championship in 1961 and 1962. For all that, Ferrari was still behind in his thinking when it came to chassis design and was outdated by the British constructors.

To strengthen his hand for 1962 Ferrari produced four more cars, two V6s of 2 and 2.8 litres and two V8s of 2.4 litres, all with single overhead camshafts per bank of cylinders. The 2- and 2.8-litre cars were respectively the 196 SP and 286 SP.

The 1962 Targa Florio saw the 196 SP in contention in the 2-litre class with Lorenzo Bandini and Giancarlo Baghetti as drivers and a new 268 SP with a 2.6-litre V8 unit driven by Phil Hill. A third entry from Maranello was a 246 SP driven by Willy Mairesse and Gendebien. Although Baghetti spun on the third lap and damaged the car his co-driver Bandini brought the 196 SP home in second place overall and first in the 2-litre class, while the 246 SP was first overall.

At the Nürburgring 1000 km race the 196 SP with Bandini at the wheel was lying fourth when, during a routine pit stop, oil was found seeping from a cracked sump plate and this caused its retirement. The car also raced at the Nassau Speed Week driven by Bob Fulp, but failed to finish.

For the second year running a 196 SP was entered for the Targa Florio. With Mairesse at the wheel it spun, damaging the rear cover. However, despite this Mairesse only lost to Bonnier's Porsche by a mere 11 secs.

The 196 SP ended its career contesting the various European hill climbs with considerable success. In 1962, for example, Ludovico Scarfiotti won at Fornova-Monte Cassio, Mont Ventoux, Monte Bondone, Freiburg Schauinsland and Ollon Villars, and Ferrari took the European Mountain Championship, beating Porsche by 11 points.

LEFT *The 206 GT designed by Pininfarina was produced between 1967 and 1969, with a mid-mounted 2-litre V6 producing 180 bhp. Kay Stubberfield owns the car.*

BELOW *The 246 GTS is the spyder version of the 246 GT designed by Pininfarina and built by Scaglietti. It was introduced at the 1972 Geneva show and was produced for two years. This car is owned and frequently raced by John Swift.*

The V6 Dino 246 GT and GTS

At the Paris Salon in October 1965 Pininfarina exhibited a road version of the Dino 206S with rear engine, designated 206 GT. Its lineage came down through the Dino 246 (1961 grand prix car) and the Dino 166P. The 1987 cc V6 engine, developing 180 bhp at 8000 rpm was mounted in unit with the transmission, transfer case and differential, and placed directly behind the driver's compartment. The bodywork styling was highly pleasing, with flowing aerodynamic lines from front to tail and the engine air scoops recessed from the doors to the front part of the rear mudguards.

The Dino 246 GT followed in the spring of 1969 and was first shown at Geneva where it made an immediate impact on the press and public. With a transverse mid-engine enlarged to 2418 cc (bore and stroke 92.5 × 60 mm) the 246 GT had a power output of 195 bhp at 7600 rpm. It had twin overhead camshafts per bank of cylinders and a five-speed all-synchromesh and reverse gearbox. The coachwork was sleek and very smooth and followed the lines of the handsome 206 GT; by 1972 a spyder version was on the market (in effect only the roof panel was removable). Both cars were built by Scaglietti. The 246 GT was marketed in direct competition with the Porsche 911 S and its derivatives although, perhaps, its performance—a top speed of 235 km/h (146 mph)—did not quite match that of the quickest versions of the German car. Nonetheless the Dino caught the imagination of the young executive and other potential buyers who had been always hankering after a Ferrari. Unhappily many of the vehicles were not looked after properly and it has been only in latter years that Ferrari enthusiasts have sought and restored these fine cars, many to concours standard. Initially sold in the UK at the comparatively low price of around £6000, many fully restored models now command a price of £11,000 or more.

The 246 GT and GTS Dino seem to have been among the very few road cars to have had praise heaped on them by motoring journalists with virtually no reservations. It could be said that the Dino 246 GT was the first attempt by the factory to have an uninterrupted series run. After five years in production it gave way to the V8 Dino 308 GT4 2 — 2, which was introduced in 1973.

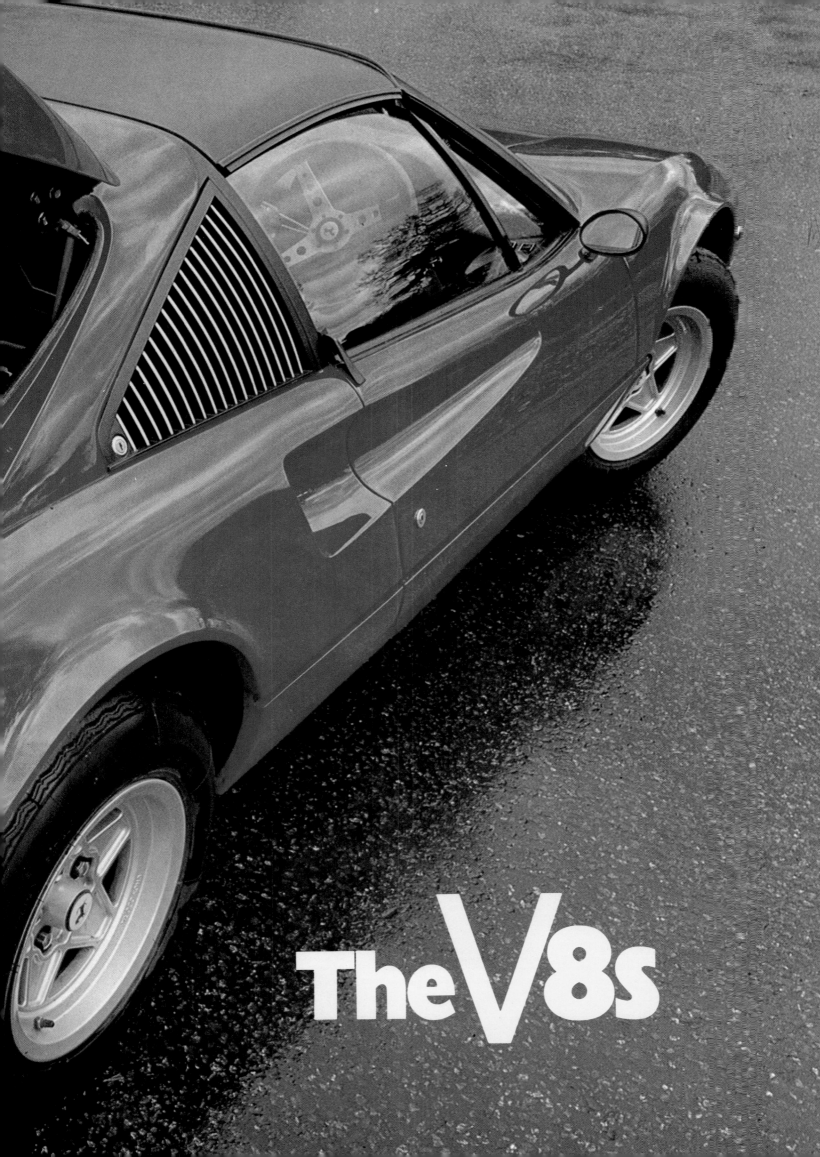

The V8s

Scuderia Ferrari was at a low ebb in 1954 after the two preceding spectacular seasons with the 500 F2 cars. The 625 F1, although reliable, lacked power and the Squalo and Supersqualo were hardly successes.

Alberto Ascari and Luigi Villoresi left the Scuderia at the start of the 1954 season, moving to Lancia where a V8-engined car was being developed for grand prix racing. The Lancia D50, however, did not make its debut until the end of the season in the Spanish GP at Barcelona, where its speed put Ascari in pole position. However, neither he nor Villoresi finished the race, although the car's performance had made it a possible contender for honours in the 1955 season.

Lancia sent five cars and three drivers to Argentina for the first race of 1955 where, once more, they showed exceptional speed but were sensitive to handle due to the concentration of weight in the centre. Modifications were carried out before the next race at Turin, which Ascari won, but at Monte Carlo he plunged into the harbour when supposedly chasing Moss in his Mercedes (Moss, in fact, had just retired).

Ascari, besides being a Lancia works driver, was contracted to drive Ferraris in sports-car racing, but he met with a fatal accident trying out a sports Ferrari at Monza a few days after his Monaco splash. This was the last straw for Lancia, which was already overstretched financially. The firm withdrew from GP racing and decided to hand over all the cars and other equipment to Ferrari, who needed a more competitive car at that time.

The D50 chassis was a multi-tubular spaceframe with the engine acted as the upper front connecting member. The fuel tanks were panniers on outriggers situated between the front and rear wheels, and there was also a fuel tank in the tail, giving in all a capacity of 205 litres (48 UK gallons). Suspension at the front was by equal-length 'A' arms, a

PAGES 36/37 *Rear view of a 308 GTS (owner, J. L. Barder) showing engine.*

.ABOVE *John Surtees in the 158 F1 follows Bandini's 512 F1 flat-12 during the 1965 Monaco GP. Surtees ran out of fuel on the penultimate lap and coasted home to fourth place. Bandini was second behind Hill's BRM.*

LEFT *Five Lancia-Ferraris contested the 1956 Monaco GP. Collins, seen here lying second on lap 54, later handed the car to Fangio who had damaged his D50. Fangio then finished second, gaining points for another championship.*

transverse leaf spring, and telescopic shock absorbers at the rear universal-jointed halfshafts were used with double parallel radius rods. A de Dion tube was behind the transmission with a transverse leaf spring below the differential casing. Telescopic shock absorbers took care of the damping. Brakes were hydraulic with finned drums and originally were of the four-shoe type, but early on they reverted to two shoes. Centre-lock Borrani wire wheels were shod with Pirelli tyres, 5.50 16 at the front and 7.00/16 at the rear. The wheelbase was 2280 mm (7 ft 6 in), the track was 1270 mm (4 ft 2 in) at both front and rear, and the weight less fuel and driver was 620 kg (1367 lb). The engine was a 90-degree four-camshaft V8 set at an angle allowing the drive shaft to pass along the near side of the driver to the rear-mounted transverse gearbox (five-speed-and-reverse) in unit with the ZF limited-slip final drive, a dry multi-plate clutch transmitting the drive. This layout gave the driver a low seat position. Bore and stroke of 73.6 mm × 73.1 mm gave a capacity of 2485 cc. The crankcase and cylinder block were of aluminium alloy with wet liners and a five-main-bearing crankshaft. The twin camshafts per bank of cylinders were chain driven and operated the two valves per cylinder. Twin magnetos driven from the rear intake of the camshaft fed the electrics to the two sparkplugs per cylinder. Four Solex 40 P11 twin-throat down-draft carburettors were located in the engine 'V' and, with a compression ratio of 11.9:1, the power output was 250 bhp at 8100 rpm.

To keep weight down a considerable amount of drilling was in evidence, for example, the steering arms, steering-wheel spokes, and the bracket holding the de Dion tube to the base of the differential casing; and the rocker arms operating the inboard shock absorbers were also drilled.

There was little time for any modifications when Scuderia Ferrari took over but Ferrari substituted Englebert tyres for the Pirellis renamed the cars Ferrari-Lancia D50s, and added his Prancing Horse insignia.

During the winter of 1955–6 the factory installed a larger fuel tank in the tail to improve handling. The exhaust pipes were realigned so that they exited through the rear lower end of the pannier tanks. At the front an anti-roll bar was added, and at the rear the leaf spring was placed above the gearbox. Telescopic shock absorbers were replaced with vane-type Houdailles and to give greater strength upper frame tubes were added to the chassis. It was not long before the pannier tanks were fused into the bodywork to give a smoother line.

By mid-1956 the D50's bore had been enlarged to 76 mm and the

Following the 246 GTs, the 308 GTB has flowing balanced lines. Shown at Paris in 1975 it had a glass-fibre body, reverting to steel in 1977. With a mid-engined 90-degree V8 3-litre unit the car can top 240 km/h (150 mph). Owned by James Marshall.

stroke was reduced to 68.5 mm giving a displacement of 2487 cc. For the French GP Castellotti's car had a fresh and pleasing look. A full-width nose with faired moulded section ahead of the front wheels was fitted together with moulded mudguard sections over the rear wheels with scoops to assist cooling of the tyres. Unfortunately the new additions did not help for, in side winds, the car became unstable and the sections were therefore removed.

For the Scuderia 1956 was a good year. It won five of the seven championship rounds, with Juan-Manuel Fangio taking the drivers' championship from Stirling Moss (Maserati) by three points (30 to 27).

For the 1957 Argentine GP a new manifold was tried, with the Solex carburettors now forming an inverted 'V' but, as no advantage was gained, the manifolding was realigned as previously. Weber carburettors were also tried but although they improved top-end power they did nothing for mid-range torque and so they were discarded. By the spring the Ferrari-Lancia 801 appeared with the slightly increased output of 275 bhp at 8200 rpm. The bore and stroke had been altered to 80 mm × 62 mm giving a capacity of 2494.8 cc, and the suspension was changed to Supersqualo-type coils. The 'A' arms were now of unequal length and telescopic shock absorbers were back. The track had been increased to

ABOVE AND INSET *Three cars were entered for the 1962 Targa Florio. Phil Hill's 268 SP (No 150) crashed in practice. A 246 SP won and a 196 SP was second, and first in the 2-litre class.*

1320 mm (4 ft 4 in) and the weight was up by 30 kg (66 lb). The chassis had larger-diameter tubes, but without the upper front tubes, and a cleaner appearance was given to the bodywork by removing the side panniers and by placing the four-branch exhaust pipes so that they discharged the gases in front of the rear tyres.

The 1957 season was not a good one for Ferrari. The 801 won minor races only although it was placed on a number of occasions. During the season the front-engined V6 Dinos were being developed and were challenging the Cooper Climax cars in Formula 2 events.

From 1957 until 1964 the racing cars were all V6s, first with front-mounted engines and then from 1960, after Ferrari had been finally convinced that the new arrangement had come to stay, with rear-mounted units.

During this period the Aero V8s (with chassis based on an aircraft design) came on the scene. Ferrari had his first monocoque chassis tested at the Modena circuit in the summer of 1963. It housed a rear-mounted 90-degree V8 unit that was designed to be a part of the chassis. With a bore and stroke of 64 × 57.8 mm it displaced 1487.5 cc and the output was 205 bhp at 10,500 rpm; fuel injection was used. A great deal of attention was paid to the streamlining at the front, and to this end the springs were set inboard and the steering linkage lined up with the upper wishbones. The aluminium seat was part of the fuel tank, with the remainder of the fuel housed in side tanks ahead of the driver. This Aero chassis was used with the V6 engine during 1963 while the V8, designated 158 F1, was being further developed for the following year. For 1964 the bore was enlarged to 67 mm and the stroke reduced to 52.8 mm. Four coils in the 'V' fed twin ignition and the injection pump was belt driven.

During 1964 development work on the boxer-12 (a 180-degree engine) went ahead with a view to the car (designated 512 F1) taking over from the 158 F1. Both machines were used during the 1965 season but successes were hard to come by.

The 158 F1 was the last V8 used by Ferrari for formula racing. Top of the current range of Ferrari V8 road cars is the magnificent 308 GTB.

Probably one of the most stylish and sleekest cars ever produced, it was designed by the master Italian coachbuilders, Pininfarina. This and the other current V8 models are discussed in more detail later.

The 248 SP and 268 SP Sports Cars

During the transitional period from front- to rear-mounted power units a great deal of experimentation was in evidence and more than a little confusion for the Ferrari historian. Outwardly it was at times difficult, if not impossible, to tell the difference between the V6- and V8-engined SP cars unless the rear cover was lifted to expose the unit to view.

The 248 SP was unveiled at Ferrari's annual press conference in early 1962. It had a 90-degree V8 engine with bore and stroke of 77 × 66 mm and a capacity of 2458 cc, a single overhead camshaft per bank of cylinders, and single ignition. The four double-choke 40 IF2C Weber carburettors were located in the 'V' and the output was 250 bhp at 7000 rpm. Its competition life was curtailed after a disappointing debut at Sebring. Stirling Moss and Innes Ireland were cowd to drive but finding the car uncompetitive during practice, decided to drive a 3-litre Testa Rossa instead. From this point the engine was enlarged to 2.6 litres by increasing the stroke to 71 mm and the output to 265 bhp.

The new 2.6-litre V8 appeared for the 1962 Targa Florio but was eliminated during practice with a badly damaged chassis when Phil Hill went off the road—claiming that the throttle had stuck. It is doubtful whether this car was rebuilt although another 268 SP, believed to be the one used by Bandini at the Le Mans trials, was raced during the Nassau Speed Week in November 1962.

The term SP has never been explained by the factory but is generally accepted as meaning Sports Prototype, as the numerically small and somewhat exclusive series, which included V6 cars, had a short life of some two years or so. However, its importance cannot be too strongly emphasized for from this prototype series came an upsurge in Ferrari fortunes and probably some of the finest racing ever seen, with such cars as the 250 P, 250 LM, the early Ps, and finally the fabulous 330 P4s.

The V12s and boxer flat 12s

Although the new Ferrari factory at Maranello had been bombed during World War 2 Enzo was prepared, when hostilities ceased, to re-enter motor racing. He had sufficient finance available and the nucleus of a team including the great automobile technician, Luigi Bazzi, with whom he had worked from the early 1920s.

Ferrari had long admired 12-cylinder engines and decided to build such cars; and, having worked with Gioacchino Colombo on the two Alfa Bimotores of 1935 and the Alfetta of 1937, he offered him the position of designer in 1946. The same year Ferrari announced that he would embark on a programme of grand prix, sports, and road cars all with a V12 unit. This made sense for it meant that with only minor modifications and some detuning, the grand prix engine could be used for three types of car.

Ferrari intended to start with the grand prix car, but the sports version was the first to take its place on a grid at a minor event at Piacenza in May 1947. The grand prix cars appeared at the Valentino Park event in September 1948 with Giuseppe Farina, Raymond Sommer, and 'Bira' as drivers. Sommer was placed third, Farina drove into a straw bale, and 'Bira' retired with transmission trouble. The car was designated Tipo 125 and had 12 cylinders in 60-degree V-formation, and bore and stroke of 55 × 52.5 mm giving a displacement of 1496.7 cc. The crankcase and cylinder blocks were of aluminium alloy with detachable heads. A single overhead camshaft per bank of cylinders was chain driven from the front operating one intake and one exhaust valve per cylinder. A single 40 DO3C carburettor placed in the 'V' of the engine fed the fuel, and a single-stage Roots-type supercharger ran at 1.22 times the crankshaft speed. Twin magnetos driven from the rear of the camshaft sparked a single 14 mm plug per cylinder. The compression ratio was 6.5:1 and the power output was 225 bhp at 7000 rpm. A five-speed 'crash' gearbox was in unit with the engine and single clutch plate, drive was via an open propshaft to a fixed final drive, and the halfshafts were exposed. The chassis was a tubular frame and the main members were oval in section; the front cross member was of box section and formed aluminium body

panels were held to a welded tubular upper structure.

The front suspension had unequal-length wishbones, a transverse leaf spring and at the rear swing axle halfshafts, single radius arms and torsion bars, which were discarded for a transverse leaf spring in 1949. Damping was by vane-type Houdaille shock absorbers and the brakes were hydraulic with finned alloy drums. The 16 in centre-lock Borrani wheels were equipped with Pirelli tyres, 5.50/16 at the front and 6.50/16 at the rear. The car had a short wheelbase of 2160 mm (7 ft 1 in), which gave it not only twitchy handling on corners but also instability on straights. The front track was 1255 mm (4 ft 2 in), the rear 1200 mm (3 ft 11 in).

Apart from its appearance at Valentino Park the Tipo 125 was entered for three other events in 1948; at a minor race at Garda, Farina drove it to first place, but at Monza and Barcelona the transmission failed.

For the 1949 Monza GP a revised car appeared, still designated 125 F1; the capacity remained as before, but with twin overhead camshafts per bank of cylinders and twin-stage supercharging, it had an increased output of 290 bhp at 7500 rpm. To counteract the earlier car's instability the wheelbase was increased to 2380 mm (7 ft 10 in) and the track was widened but handling, although improved, was still far from satisfactory. However, thanks to the absence from racing of the Alfa Romeo team, the 125 F1 was dominant and had a successful season.

During the early postwar period there were two other formulae available for racing-car constructors, namely Formule Libre and Formula 2, and for such events the early basic design of the 125 came in useful. In 1949 the 166 Formule Libre car made its debut using the basic short-chassis 125 parts, but with a bore and stroke of 60 × 58.8 mm displacing 1995 cc. For 1950 the car used the long-wheelbase chassis and in each case a single Weber 40 DORC carburettor was employed. For F2 races the 166 discarded the single-stage blower but used three 32 DCF Weber carburettors, and its output with a 10:1 compression ratio was 155 bhp at 7000 rpm. By late 1950 the 166 F2 had a four-speed-and-reverse gearbox in unit with the ZF limited-slip final drive and double parallel radius rods added. The bodywork was also revised with a wider but

This is the privately owned 1951 Formula 1 car campaigned by Peter Whitehead in Europe and entered in a few races by the works with some success. At one period, when in Australia, it was raced with a Chevrolet V8 engine. In 1964 Tom Wheatcroft, owner of Donington racing car museum, bought this 125 F1 (chassis 114) from an Australian owner and by 1973 it was completely restored.

narrower grille giving an overall sleeker appearance. There was also a de Dion version of the car. The 166 F2 had a good and successful run, winning 13 out of 15 Formula 2 races during 1950.

By 1950 Colombo had departed and Lampredi had taken over to design and develop a larger-capacity non-supercharged V12, and then to prepare a 2.5-litre four-cylinder unit for F1 racing in 1954. One reason behind the change in design policy was a particular difficulty his cars increasingly had to contend with on the circuits. While other constructors' cars with their non-supercharged engines could finish a race without a pit stop for refuelling, Ferrari's blown cars lost valuable time by having to take on more fuel, thereby reducing their chances of winning. Ferrari was also aware that Alfa Romeo was updating its cars for a return to the circuits in 1951 and it was one of his ambitions to defeat them, believing that he alone was able to achieve this distinction. He felt, no doubt, that the 125 design had reached the peak of its performance and little was to be gained by trying to extract any further power.

The first of the larger-capacity cars was the 1950 275 F1 3.3-litre 60-degree V12 which was used as a test bed for what followed. This was the 340 F1 with an increase in capacity to 4.1 litres, and then came the 375 F1 with a bore and stroke of 80 × 74.5 mm displacing 4493.7 cc. The chassis and suspension, except for minor modifications, followed the original Colombo-designed cars, but with a de Dion tube as standard practice and a longer wheelbase. The 275 F1 had twin magnetos driven from the rear of the camshaft and a single sparkplug, as did the early 375, but this was changed in 1951 to a single magneto driven from the front and two plugs per cylinder. The final output was 380 bhp at 7500 rpm—although the

375 Formule Libre car was boosted to 390 bhp.

The 1951 season was reasonably successful for the 375 F1, which won three championship rounds against the highly competitive Alfa Romeos, but Ferrari came unstuck in the final round, the Spanish GP at Pedralbes, where incorrect tyre selection lost the company the race and also the manufacturers' championship. The Alfa Romeo concern having accomplished what it had set out to prove, that its cars were still the best, pulled out and put the dust sheets over the machines. This virtually put paid to Formula 1 racing for some years as Ferrari had no opposition for his cars except for limited opportunities in Formule Libre, and later a half-hearted attempt at testing them against the specialized American machines on their home ground at Indianapolis.

The 375 was a handsome car with the bodywork following closely that of the 166 models with their narrower and bulbous grille, whereas the 125 had ended up with a large, arched waffle-like grille. In addition the factory built a variant of the 375 designated 412 M1 with a smaller-capacity engine of 4023.2 cc using six Weber 42 DCN carburettors and a healthy output of 430 bhp at 7800 rpm. Most of these cars found homes in the United States when they were sold.

From 1951 to 1963 Ferrari was involved with the in-line four, in-line six and V6 and also the V8 cars that he acquired from Lancia. It was not until 1964 that he reverted to 12 cylinders for the premier division, although the V12 units continued to power a number of highly competitive and successful GT and sports-racing cars.

In 1964 the first of the 180-degree flat-12 cars appeared, the 512 F1 with a displacement of 1489.6 cc (bore and stroke 56 × 30.4 mm) and Lucas fuel injection. Four coils and distributors sparked a single plug per cylinder (the 1965 car had two plugs per cylinder) and the output was 220 bhp at 11,500 rpm (increased by 5 bhp for the 1965 car). The engine used the 158 F1 monocoque chassis and similar suspension, and although driven by Bandini in practice for the Italian GP at Monza it was not considered fully tested and so did not race. Its racing debut came at the United States GP at Watkins Glen in the same year, driven by Bandini, but it was retired. The Ferrari team, at Watkins Glen and also at Mexico City for the Mexican GP, ran under the North American Racing Team banner as Enzo was, at the time, in dispute with the Italian racing authorities. Also, he not only had the 512 F1 but also other team cars (John Surtees' 158 F1 and, in addition, the 156 F1 for Pedro Rodriguez at Mexico City) repainted in the United States international racing colours of blue and white.

Although the 512 F1 was reliable and finished in most races it contested, it could not be said to have distinguished itself during the two seasons of its career.

The Fédération Internationale de l'Automobile (FIA) introduced the 3-litre unsupercharged and 1.5-litre supercharged capacities for Formula 1 from 1966. Few constructors had a machine ready but Ferrari managed to field one car for Surtees for the first European event at Syracuse which he won from Bandini using a Dino V6.

Ferrari reverted to the well-tried 60-degree V12 unit, but mounted at the rear for the new formula, and left the design to Ing. Franco Rocchi. The main features were Lucas high-pressure fuel injection between the cylinder banks, two sparkplugs per cylinder ignited by four coils and twin distributors, and two valves per cylinder. The chassis was still monocoque with the body/chassis of riveted aluminium sheets formed round steel tubes, and the engine was used as part of the rear chassis member. The rubber fuel tanks were carried on each side of the cockpit.

The front suspension used upper rocker arms, wide base 'A' arms and inboard coil springs and shock-absorber units. At the rear universal-jointed halfshafts were employed, together with reversed lower 'A' arms, single upper links, coil spring and shock absorber. The long radius rods were not parallel but the upper one was adjustable. At the front the Girling disc brakes were mounted outboard, but inboard at the rear, and the wheels were either 14 in bolt-on or centre-lock cast magnesium alloy five-spoke or slotted-disc Campagnolos shod with Dunlops. A multi-plate clutch was placed between the engine and the gearbox, which was five-speed-and-reverse in unit with the final drive.

During the years 1966 to 1969, as development of the unit progressed, a number of modifications were carried out. The 24-valve engine by the end of 1966 had 36 valves (2 intake/1 exhaust) and from late 1967 until the end of the series (designated 312 F1) 48 valves (2 intake/2 exhaust). Other changes concerned sizes of wheels, and the Dunlop tyres were replaced by Firestones from 1967. From an initial bhp of 360 at 10,000 rpm the final unit produced 436 bhp at 11,000 rpm. The wing or rear aerofoil pioneered by Richie Ginther in 1961, which improved the stability of the 246 SP, was used on the early 1968 car mounted on struts; this innovation in a variety of forms has been part of all today's racing cars.

The 312 F1 had a far from outstanding race history. During the first two years it proved reasonably reliable but during 1968 and 1969 there were too many retirements (although for trivial reasons). It appeared that the day of the V12 as a competitive racing unit was nearly over, and that both Chris Amon and Jacky Ickx, as drivers, were unfortunate in being 'in' at the tail end, although Amon came close to winning at least three GPs.

Not one to be discouraged when fortunes were at low ebb, Ferrari started on a comeback in 1970 with the boxer flat-12, which owed much to the knowledge gained from the 512 F1 and the 212 E sports car, campaigned by Peter Schetty in 1969, which had wiped the board clean in the European Hill Climb Championship. The start to the season was encouraging but no more, but fortunes picked up with the German GP at Hockenheim where Ickx was placed second. From the last five grands prix of the season the 312B F1 gained four firsts, and on three occasions a one/two with Swiss driver Regazzoni following the team leader home.

There was early encouragement in 1971 up to the time of the Dutch GP, with five first places including the Brands Hatch Race of Champions. However, the remainder of the season brought too many retirements, caused on some occasions by engine failure. Both the 312 B and B2 cars were used and it was the latter that was producing the major problems. The following year only the B2 was raced and once more it was an 'also-ran', even though many of the problems of the previous season had been ironed out and it did prove reasonably reliable, retiring less frequently. The 1973 season was the mixture as before: the B3 car, driven by Ickx, appeared at the Spanish GP at Montjuich Park, Barcelona, on 29 April but claimed only 12th place, and it failed to provide Maranello with any successes.

It should be remembered that during this period the factory was more than stretched trying to win the World Championship for Makes for sports-racing cars with the 312 PB, which used a similar but detuned boxer flat-12, for these races were endurance tests and not the comparative sprints of approx 200 miles covered by the GP cars.

By late 1974 the new T series boxer (T standing for Transversale, meaning transverse gearbox) was shown to the press and in its first season (1975) gave Niki Lauda the drivers' world championship and Ferrari the manufacturers' award.

In 1976 Lauda continued his successful run, winning the Brazilian, South African, Belgian and Monaco Grands Prix. However, at the German GP at the Nürburgring he was very seriously injured in a horrific accident, and it was only his remarkable will to live that pulled him through. Amazingly, he was back behind the wheel for the last three grands prix of the season, gaining valuable points in each, and ensuring that Ferrari won the manufacturers' award.

Driving the 312 T2, Lauda was back in action in 1977 and, although he won only three grands prix (the South African, German and Dutch), he had been placed so many times during the season that he secured the drivers' championship, Ferrari also taking the manufacturers' title again.

The 312 Ts are now in their fifth series (T5) and are proving not only reliable but extremely fast, picking up their fair share of the grand prix spoils in the hands of the South African Jody Scheckter and the French-Canadian Gilles Villeneuve, with Scheckter securing the 1979 drivers' title

Tipo 312 T2 (1976)		
ENGINE		**CHASSIS**
Type Original design by Forghieri, Rocchi and Bussi. Flat-12 boxer		**Frame** Monocoque and additional tubular frame at front of cockpit
No. of cylinders 12		**Wheelbase mm** 2560
Bore/stroke mm 80.0 × 49.6		**Track – front mm** 1400
Displacement cc 2991		**rear mm** 1430
Valve operation Twin overhead cam per bank of cyls		**Suspension – front** Long upper rocker arms, angled inboard coil springs
Ignition Marelli transistor		
Sparkplugs per cyl. 1		**rear** Narrow based reversed lower 'A' arms. Upper radius rods only
Compression ratio 11.8:1		
Carburation Lucas fuel injection		
BHP 500 at 12,200 rpm		**Shock absorbers** Angled inboard units
		Brakes Lockheed discs
DRIVE TRAIN		**Tyre size – front** 9.20/20.00
Clutch Dry multi-plate		**rear** 14.00/26.00
Transmission Five-speed-and-reverse gearbox mounted transversely behind engine in unit with final drive		**Wheels** 13-inch cast magnesium alloy. Four-spoke front, disc at rear.
		Performance Max speed 180 mph, 0–
		(approx) 60 mph 3 sec, standing quarter mile 9 sec
Rear axle Universal jointed halfshafts, anti-roll bar		

at Monza. The specifications for the T2 are set out elsewhere, together with those of other models that are considered important in the marque's history. For 1980 minor modifications have been made with a redesigned head to enhance airflow and ground effects, revised front and rear suspensions and brakes, with improved bodywork aerodynamics.

The 3-litre boxer-12s have been on the circuits since 1969: the 312 T has proved reliable and the 'ground-effect' skirts (pioneered by the Lotus 79) give greater stability and therefore better performance.

As far as the body was concerned the first B cars followed the pattern of all the rear-engined machines; they looked sleek and it was still possible to distinguish one marque from another, apart from colour. Thereafter the cars could hardly be described as aesthetically appealing, especially when the high air intake behind the driver's compartment was in vogue. As with the aerofoils on struts, which had to be modified, the racing authorities banned the high intake for all 1976 cars; once again they took on a smooth aerodynamic line, after the ban became effective halfway through the season.

One other important factor, from the late 1950s, was tyre sizes; first

the rear tyres were widened and then both the front and rear, with the rear ones becoming almost grotesque in appearance. About the same time it was realized more than ever before that it was necessary to have the cars correctly shod for wet, intermediate or dry conditions, and that the various surfaces over which racing took place demanded a variety of compounds, and that these in turn required the correct setting up of the car's suspension.

The spyders and berlinettas
As has been seen, Enzo Ferrari's first production models under his own name were the V12 Tipo 125 cars. Three were built but initially only one retained the 1500 cc engine; the others were first bored out to 1902 cc and called Tipo 159, but in 1948 all three were enlarged to 1995 cc and designated Tipo 166.

They had somewhat crude but adequate bodywork, two seats, cycle-type wings and headlamps. However, the wings and lamps were removable so that the machines could be used for formula racing as well as participating in sports-car events. They were fast, reliable and well able to outclass machines of far greater capacities. It is not surprising, therefore, that they had many successes, including long-distance races. It was not long before an all-enveloping body, by Carrozzeria Touring, clothed the chassis, giving a most pleasing appearance, and one early car fitted with a coupé top and driven by Clemente Biondetti won the 1948 Mille Miglia. In honour of this victory all 166 models thereafter had the affix MM after the numbers.

It is important to remember that the original chassis, engine, and design of many parts formed the basis for most models, with modifications, until the mid-1960s. There were a number of variants based on the 166, such as the 212 produced as the Export or Sport with a short wheelbase, and the Inter with a longer wheelbase—this was basically a road version although used in competition. There was also the 195, built with berlinetta and spyder coachwork, and it was not always easy to differentiate between the 166, 212, and 195.

Ferrari's first big sports car was announced in the summer of 1950 and the same year the model 340 America appeared at the Paris Salon. The Lampredi-designed long-block engine of 4101.6 cc (bore and stroke, 80 × 68 mm) powered the car, which had an output of 220 bhp at 6000 rpm and a claimed top speed of 220 km/h (137 mph). There were

two other versions, the 340 MM and 340 Mexico. Although this Tipo had a number of successes in Europe, including the long-distance Mille Miglia, it was intended for the United States market and campaigned successfully in a variety of events by American drivers.

During 1952 and 1953 Ferrari sports cars were dominant and the factory competed with five different capacity cars, the 2-litre 166 MM, the 2.3-litre 195 S, the 2.7-litre 225 S, the 3-litre 250 Sport, and the 4.1-litre 340 MM and Mexico. The 250 Sport or MM was insufficiently developed, although it had shown promise, but Ferrari had by then turned his attention to the 4.5-litre 375.

The 1953 Le Mans event provided the first outing for a 375 MM berlinetta but, after setting a new lap record, it retired with clutch trouble; two 340 MM berlinettas were also entered and these cars, after the race, were brought up to the 375 specification so that the three cars and a Vignale-bodied 375 MM spyder formed the Ferrari team for the remainder of the year. For 1954 the factory relied on the new 375 Plus which was modified and had more power than the 375 MM. The 84 mm bore was retained but it had a 74.5 mm stroke displacing 4954.3 cc, and with three twin-choke 46 DCF3 Weber carburettors it had a bhp rating of 344 at 6500 rpm.

Tipo 375 MM (1954)	
ENGINE	
Type	Lampredi-designed, water-cooled 60-degree V12
No. of cylinders	12
Bore/stroke mm	84.0 × 68.0
Displacement cc	4522
Valve operation	Single overhead cams per bank of cyls
Ignition	Two Marelli magnetos
Sparkplugs per cyl.	1
Compression ratio	9.0:1
Carburation	Three Weber 40 IF4C four-choke, downdraft
BHP	340 at 7000 rpm
DRIVE TRAIN	
Clutch	Multiple disc
Transmission	Four-speed all-synchromesh, reverse, direct drive in 4th
Rear axle	Live
CHASSIS	
Frame	Welded tubular steel ladder type
Wheelbase mm	2600
Track – front mm	1325
rear mm	1320
Suspension – front	Unequal-length 'A' arms, transverse leaf, anti-roll bar
rear	Live axle semi-elliptical springs, parallel trailing arms
Shock absorbers	Houdaille hydraulic, lever action
Brakes	Hydraulic, aluminium drums, iron liners
Tyre size – front	6.00 × 16
rear	7.00 × 16
Wheels	Borrani wire, centre-lock, knock-off
Performance (approx)	Max speed 160 mph, 0–60 mph 7 sec, standing quarter mile 12 sec

Tipo 166 Corsa Spyder (1948)	
ENGINE	
Type	Colombo-designed, water-cooled 60-degree V12
No. of cylinders	12
Bore/stroke mm	60.0 × 58.8
Displacement cc	1995
Valve operation	Single overhead cam per bank of cyls
Ignition	Two Marelli magnetos
Sparkplugs per cyl.	1
Compression ratio	10.0:1
Carburation	Three Weber 30 DCF twin-choke, downdraft
BHP	150 at 7000 rpm
DRIVE TRAIN	
Clutch	Single dry plate
Transmission	Five-speed non-synchromesh and reverse, direct drive in 4th
Rear axle	Live
CHASSIS	
Frame	Welded tubular steel
Wheelbase mm	2420
Track – front mm	1278
rear mm	1200
Suspension – front	Independent, unequal-length 'A' arms, transverse leaf
rear	Live axle, semi-elliptical springs, parallel trailing arms
Shock absorbers	Dubonnet hydraulic, lever action
Brakes	Hydraulic, aluminium drums, iron liners
Tyre size – front	5.90 × 15
rear	5.90 × 15
Wheels	Borrani wire, centre-lock, knock-off
Performance (approx)	Max speed 125 mph, 0–60 mph 10 sec, standing quarter mile 16 sec

ABOVE *This beautifully proportioned 212 Barchetta is owned by John Briggs and Don Nelson. The 212s had a distinguished racing history*

ABOVE LEFT *Built for long-distance races, the 1953 375 MM needed muscle to drive. This beautifully styled car belongs to R. Cederlund*

LEFT *The 1948 166 Corsa Spyder (owner, P. Jackman).*

March 1952 should be a month savoured by all true Ferrari enthusiasts for on the first day a prototype front-engined 3-litre V12 unit was being road-tested which, if it proved itself (and it did), was to be the power source of probably the most famous series of cars to grace the automobile world both as road and racing machines. This was the advent of the 250 series which set Ferrari on the road to success and established not only his name but also his reputation as a constructor of high-performance cars. During the first five years a trickle of no more than about 200 machines had been built, but by 1963 the factory had turned out nearly 3,500 cars. The 3-litre unit was to power the 250 Europa; the Tipo will be discussed below in the section on the GT road cars.

Starting with the 1956 season the Fédération Internationale de l'Automobile established specific classes for gran turismo cars and Ferrari, having built and raced berlinettas since 1950, was in a strong position to meet any new regulations. He had unveiled two different body styles on the new 3-litre 250 GT at the 1955 Paris and Turin shows respectively, and these Pininfarina designs were 'translated' into coachwork for the cars to be built by Scaglietti and raced not only by the factory but also by customers in 1956 and for many years afterwards, showing a complete supremacy over all other GT cars. Although built initially for competition, these were also road cars even though the coachwork was light and fragile.

The factory designated all the series under a single nomenclature, 250 GT, but there were in reality three variants: the Tour de France or long-wheelbase cars, the SWB or short wheelbase, and the GTC

ABOVE *The 1949 195 S had a bored-out version of the Tipo 166 engine. A classic of its time, the coachwork was by Carrozzeria Touring.* ABOVE RIGHT *The 1950 195 Inter. Both owned by Peter Agg/Trojan Ltd.*

RIGHT *The 410 Superamerica reflects the influence of American styling. Owned by Peter Agg/Trojan Ltd, it was shown at the 1956 Paris Salon.*

The long-wheelbase 250 GTs had been in production since 1954 but were not known as the Tour de France car until 1956, when the Marquis Alfonso de Portago came in first overall and first in class in the classic long-distance French event. There were six variations from 1956 to 1959 and the different cars may be identified by alterations to the bodywork during this period.

The SWB or short-wheelbase cars were developed from the Tour de France series and the factory had in mind not only competition, but greater customer comfort by means of a superior interior trim, a detuned engine and a smoother ride from a modified suspension. Some of the cars were built with steel bodies, giving greater strength.

The GTO was the final development of the 250 GT competition berlinetta. The suffix 'O' denoted its homologation (*omologato*) within the framework of the regulations concerning the minimum numbers built by the factory; there had been a dispute between Ferrari and the race authorities on the subject. While all cars in the 250 GT series (competition and road) can be identified as such, there were, as indicated, some modifications from year to year but all were smooth in line with a purposeful look that clearly implied a race-bred design. The GTO, however, was the car that has caught the imagination of the Ferrari enthusiast, with its aerodynamic lines and, in its final production form, an upswept spoiler effect blending with the tail. The first GTO was shown to the press in February 1962, although development work had been started towards the end of 1960, and the last three cars of the series, which, using the 4-litre unit as installed in the 1960 400 Superamerica road

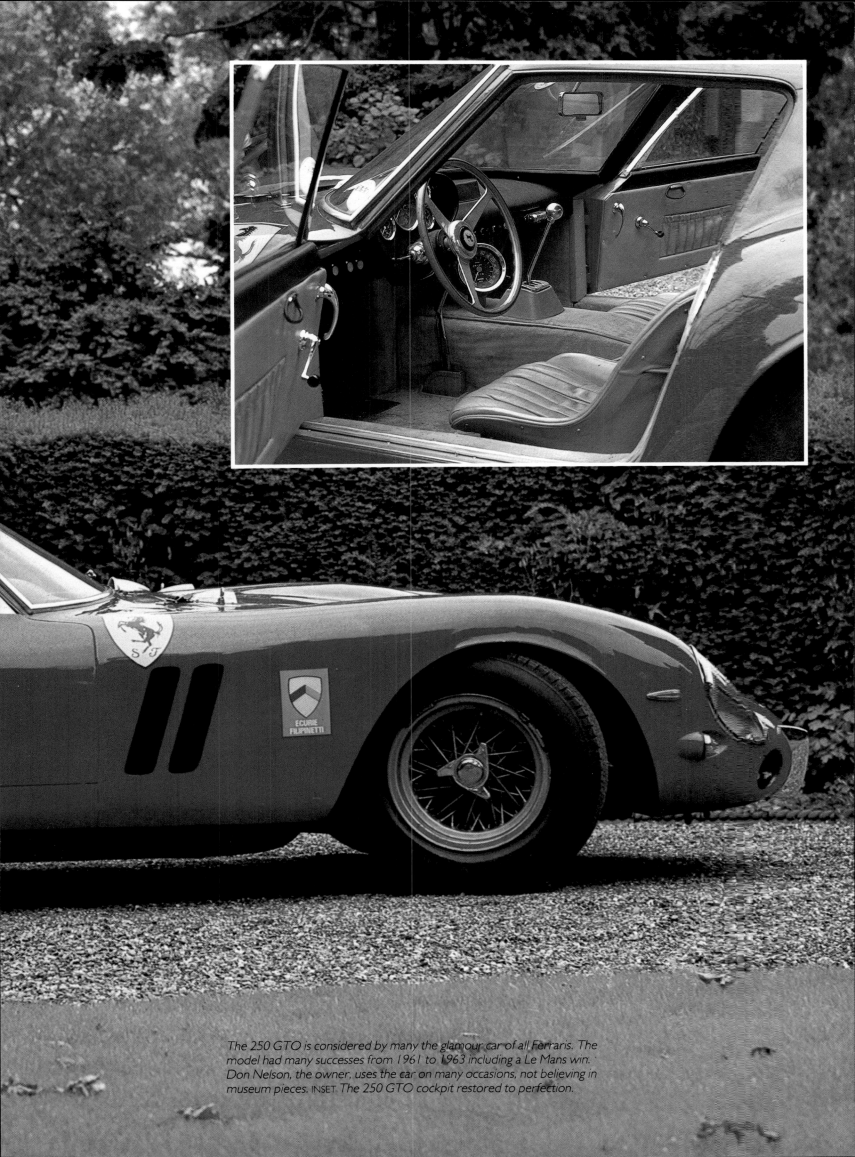

The 250 GTO is considered by many the glamour car of all Ferraris. The
model had many successes from 1961 to 1963 including a Le Mans win.
Don Nelson, the owner, uses the car on many occasions, not believing in
museum pieces. INSET The 250 GTO cockpit restored to perfection.

Tipo 250 Testa Rossa (1958)	
ENGINE	
Type	Colombo-designed, water-cooled, 60-degree V12
No. of cylinders	12
Bore/stroke mm	73.0 × 58.8
Displacement cc	2953
Valve operation	Single overhead cam per bank of cyls
Ignition	Two Marelli distributors
Sparkplugs per cyl.	1
Compression ratio	9.8:1
Carburation	Six Weber 38 DCN twin-choke, downdraft
BHP	300 at 7200 rpm
DRIVE TRAIN	
Clutch	Single dry plate
Transmission	Four-speed all-synchromesh, reverse, direct drive in 4th
Rear axle	Live
CHASSIS	
Frame	Welded tubular steel
Wheelbase mm	2350
Track – front mm	1308
rear mm	1300
Suspension – front	Independent, unequal-length 'A' arms, coil springs
rear	Live axle, semi-elliptical springs, parallel trailing arms
Shock absorbers	Houdaille hydraulic, lever action
Brakes	Hydraulic, aluminium drums, iron liners
Tyre size – front	5.50 × 16
rear	6.00 × 16
Wheels	Borrani wire, centre-lock, knock-off
Performance (approx)	Max speed 130 mph, 0–60 mph 5.8 sec, standing quarter mile 13.3 sec

RIGHT *The 250 Testa Rossa was one of the works most successful sports-racing cars, and was raced between 1958 and 1962. Owned by the Harrisons. The V12 engine is shown above.*

ABOVE RIGHT *Vic Norman's short-wheelbase 1959 250 GT.*

	Tipo 250 GT (1961)	
	ENGINE	
Type	Colombo-designed, water-cooled, 60-degree V12	
No. of cylinders	12	
Bore/stroke mm	73.0 x 58.8	
Displacement cc	2953	
Valve operation	Single overhead cam per bank of cyls	
Ignition	Two distributors	
Sparkplugs per cyl.	1	
Compression ratio	9.3	
Carburation	Three Weber DCL3 twin-choke, downdraft	
BHP	280 at 7000 rpm	
	DRIVETRAIN	
Clutch	Single dry plate	
Transmission	Four-speed all-synchromesh, reverse, direct drive in 4th	
Rear axle	Live	
	CHASSIS	
Frame	V-section tubular steel, door tree	
Wheelbase mm	2400	
Track – front mm	1354	
rear mm	1349	
Suspension – front	Coil springs unequal-length A-arms, anti-roll bar	
rear	Live axle semi-elliptical springs, parallel trailing arms	
Shock absorbers	telescopic hydraulic	
Brakes	Disc	
Tyre size – front	5.00 x 16	
rear	5.00 x 16	
Wheels	Borrani wire, centre-lock, knock-off	
Performance	Max speed 145 mph, 0–50 mph 6 sec, standing quarter mile 16 sec	
(approx)		

cars, appeared in 1964. The demise of the series in serious racing was not the end of the factory's highly successful competitive run, for other cars were in the pipeline and ready to keep the name Ferrari in the headlines.

It has already been seen that Ferrari was late in accepting the idea of a mid- or rear-engined car and that the first of these was the V6 246 F1, driven by Richie Ginther at the Monaco GP in 1960, while the 250 GT series had front-mounted units. In 1961 some organizers of long-distance races felt it necessary to continue with prototype cars and in November 1962 Ferrari unveiled his V12 3-litre mid-engined GT car, the 250 P. This was a highly successful competition car, even though only in limited production and therefore lasting for a short period. It was the forerunner of the 250 LM berlinetta, which the FIA considered to be a prototype whereas the factory felt it was a production GT. Perhaps only 40 were built, one car having a 3-litre unit (acceptable as a contender for the 1962 championship for GT cars as the upper capacity limit was 3 litres), the remainder having 3.3-litre engines and considered by many as 275 LMs.

Two other cars of the period, raced at Le Mans and elsewhere, were the 330 LMB and the front-engined 330 TR/LM Spyder, which was not a particularly good-looking car and had a twin-nostril front end.

The first Ferraris to bear the name Testa Rossa (derived from a special red finish on the camshaft covers) were the 500 TR with a 2-litre four-cylinder engine and the 500 TRCs built for customer use and also competition in 1956 and 1957. For 1957 Ferrari had to prepare cars for the 1958 World Sports Car Championship confined to an upper limit of 3 litres and, as the 250 GT 3-litre units were well in contention in competition, this engine was chosen for further development and used in the 250 TRs. The 250 Testa Rossa had an illustrious career, winning a great variety of races and carrying off the championship spoils in 1958, 1960 and 1961. A normal-bodied sports car of the period, it resembled the factory Tipo 315 Sport (3.7-litre) and 335 Sport (4-litre), derived from the 290 S (3.4-litre) with a single overhead camshaft per bank of cylinders.

The first car of the new series was seen at the 1957 Nürburgring 1000 km race where it was placed tenth. In the same season for the Le Mans event a revised 3.1-litre TR appeared with a handsome but somewhat unconventional bodywork. The front wings were cut away behind the wheels and the low-slung nose was ahead of the front line of the wings; the Tipo is known universally as either the 'pontoon'- or 'sponson'-fendered body. Both the foregoing were prototypes and the production car was shown to the press in November 1957.

The Testa Rossas' first race in the 1958 World Sports Car Championship was at Buenos Aires on 26 January where they were placed first, second and fourth. The success continued with wins at Sebring and Targa Florio and, although Moss in his Aston Martin won at the Nürburgring, the Ferrari team took the next four places. The last race in the series was at Le Mans where the Hill/Gendebien car took the chequered flag, with privately entered Ferraris coming sixth and seventh. Ferrari thus took the championship for 1958, but in the following year nothing seemed to go right for the team.

However, in 1960 the team just managed to scrape home to win the title, and while the factory had a new contender for honours in 1961 (the V6 Tipo 246 Sport), it was the Testa Rossas which enabled Ferrari to win the championship for the third time.

For the 1964 competition season Ferrari relied on two new versions of the rear-mounted V12 prototype engines, the 275 P with a 3.3-litre unit and a 4-litre engine for the Tipo 330 P. Some of the 275 P cars were probably re-engined 250 Ps, but the 330 P had a new style of bodywork.

RIGHT *The 250 LM (1963 and 1964) was raced by private entrants at Le Mans, and won there in 1965 in the hands of Gregory and Rindt. This example is owned by Mark Tippetts.*

BELOW *David Clarke's 330 P4 1967 prototype championship car.*

Tipo 330 P4 (1967)			
ENGINE		**CHASSIS**	
Type	Rocchi-designed, water-cooled, 60-degree V12	Frame	Multi-tubular
		Track – front mm	184
No. of cylinders	12, mid-engine	rear mm	183
Bore/stroke mm	77.0 × 71.0	Suspension – front	Independent, unequal wishbones, coil springs, anti-roll bar
Displacement cc	3967		
Valve operation	Twin overhead camshafts per bank of cyls	rear	Independent, one wishbone, coil springs, anti-roll bar
Ignition	Two distributors, two coils	Tyre size – front	4.75/10.30 × 15
		rear	6.00/12.30 × 15
Sparkplugs per cyl.	2	Wheels	5-spoke cast alloy
Compression ratio	11.0:1	Performance	Max. speed 200 mph.
Carburation	Lucas indirect injection	(approx)	0–60 mph 5.6 sec, standing quarter mile 13 sec
BHP	450 at 11,000 rpm		

Three of the latter cars made their debut in the Daytona 1000 km in the United States: the one driven by Surtees/Bandini took third place, the Maranello Concessionaires car (Graham Hill/Bonnier) retired after nine hours' racing after holding second position, and the third went out with a broken hose. Two of the 275 Ps were first and second. In the 1964 Le Mans 24-hour event second and third places went to the 330 Ps, the 275 P claiming another victory, but the 330 Ps had a fair share of the spoils during the remainder of the year.

A new spyder in the P series had been developed for 1965 with a wind tunnel-tested sleek body giving a low nose profile, and with diplane spoilers attached to either side to keep the front end from lifting at high speed. There were other important improvements to the body which had not, for once, been designed by the coachbuilder Pininfarina who had had a hand in all the previous sports-racing spyders. In addition to the new P2 cars there was to be a proliferation of other prototypes for the season, which must have kept the factory very much on its toes. After a poor start

The 512 M contested CanAm and other prototype races in 1970 and 1971. It was never a serious contender as its development was curtailed. Robert Horne's car holds the UK 1 km flying start record at 199·9 mph.

in America the P2 and other cars began to find their form at the Monza 1000 km race, but in general the factory P2s were not a success and the 1966 season was beset by a variety of problems such as the lack of preparation of the cars due to industrial unrest in Italy. A further blow was the resignation of John Surtees from the team after an argument with team manager Dragoni during practice for the Le Mans race.

In 1964 and 1965 the might of the Ford empire pitted itself against the other contenders for the prototype crown but on each occasion was repulsed. However, with Ferrari having problems in 1966, the door was wide open and, although Porsche took the honours, the 7-litre Fords were still a potential threat to the ordered pattern of the past.

Enzo Ferrari was nevertheless a determined man and he set about preparing for what was likely to prove a titanic struggle in 1967. Although the factory had always been adept at producing new cars and engines for a particular race or series of races, it was always slow to introduce new concepts from outside sources even though these might have been proved. The P4, to be introduced for 1967, was entirely new and the chassis did not conform to the accepted monocoque or stretched-skin construction, but relied on its torsional strength from a variety, indeed multitude, of tubes to support the many other vital accessories. It was not,

however, a spaceframe in accepted terms. Franco Rocchi designed the new engine, a mid-engine V12 with twin overhead camshafts per bank of cylinders and three valves per cylinder (2 inlet/1 exhaust); displacement was 3967 cc and bhp 450 at 11,000 rpm. It was a handsome, smooth-lined car giving an impression of enormous potential and power which, indeed, it had. Only three cars were built, for the fourth car used during the season was a P3 with the P4 power plant. Although the Fords won at Le Mans the P4s took the prototype title by 2 points from Porsche and by 12 from Ford.

The P4 was the end of a long era for the Ferrari sports racing machines, for the cars from the factory that followed in its wheel tracks conformed to the practices of its rivals.

The ruling body of automobile sport decreed that the 1968 manufacturers' championship would be contested by cars with a 3-litre limit, which certainly did not suit Ferrari: he did not have a suitable car and it was the first time since 1953, when the sports-car championship was instituted, that he was not a contestant. This is not to say that Ferraris did not compete, as a number of privateers contested races. The racing department, however, was not dormant for, apart from running the Formula 1 cars, it produced a 6-litre car for the last event of the CanAm sports car series in Canada and the USA (although token assistance was given in subsequent years, Ferrari's interest was not really serious here). At the end of the year Ferrari showed his 3-litre prototype for the 1969 championship, the 312 P with a 2990 cc V12 unit with 48 valves, Lucas injection and an output of 420 bhp at 9800 rpm. The bodywork was a scaled-down version of the CanAm car and certainly one of the most beautiful sports-racing cars ever turned out by the factory but, even when running as a berlinetta, it was a failure. It had promised so much, but after six events the dust sheets went on.

In the meantime the 512 cars, mainly in private hands but with some factory support, continued to contest the CanAm races without success. They also contested the European sports-car championship but were no match for the reliable Porsches, which could concentrate on the series without other commitments.

Ferrari was more concerned with his new project for 1971, the flat-12-engined 312 PB to be used in the manufacturers' championship; the unit was derived from the grand prix cars. In fact it could be described as a Formula 1 car with full-width two-seat bodywork that was a small and simple spyder design. The chassis was the usual tubular structure and the bodywork, in two sections, of glass fibre with water radiators situated in the centre of the chassis on either side of the cockpit. The aperture in the nose was not the air intake (these were recessed into the doors) but was for keeping the front end on the track, and at the tail end a full-width wing was held in position by two small fins. Detuned for long-distance events the 2991 cc unit produced 440 bhp at 10,800 rpm (the F1 output was 460 bhp).

Two cars were available for 1971 and one was sent for the opening championship round to Buenos Aires with Ignazio Giunti and Arturo Merzario as drivers, but when lying second Giunti, unable to take avoiding action, ran into a Matra being pushed along the track. The Ferrari burst into flames, becoming a total wreck, and the driver died of head injuries and burns. The season was one of unfortunate incidents for the remaining car with Jacky Ickx as number one driver and his co-pilot either Clay Regazzoni or Mario Andretti. It had shown its potential by being placed on the front row of the grid for most of the events entered and leading at some stage in its races before retiring, crashing or 'running out of road'.

An all-out effort was planned for 1972 and six cars were built. The idea was to have three cars always race-prepared while three would be at the works to receive any necessary attention before their next outing. The experience gained during 1971 meant that a variety of modifications needed to be carried out during the winter. The result was that the 1972 cars were more than a match for the opposition and carried off the honours without having to contest the 24-hour race at Le Mans as Ferrari decided that the 312 PB was incapable of lasting the distance.

The 1973 season was hard fought against the fast and much-improved V12 Matras and the 2.7-litre Porsche Carreras which had entered the fray. Ferrari lost to the Matras by 124 to 115 points and decided to abandon sports-car racing and concentrate on Formula 1 for the future: a wise decision as it proved.

Developed from the 312 P V12, the 1971 312 PB had a flat-12 unit, hence the 'B' for boxer. It was built for the manufacturers' championship series, winning the title in 1972. The car is shown during the 1971 BOAC 1000 at Brands Hatch.

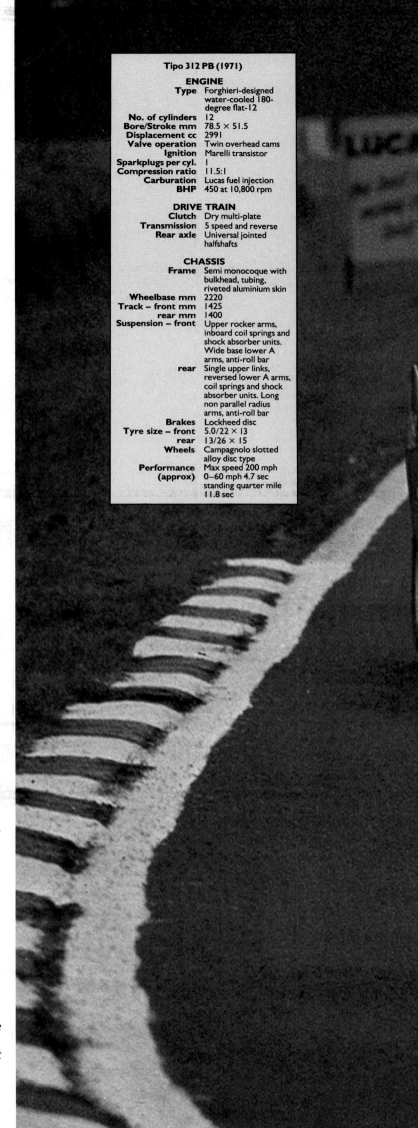

Tipo 312 PB (1971)	
ENGINE	
Type	Forghieri-designed water-cooled 180-degree flat-12
No. of cylinders	12
Bore/Stroke mm	78.5 × 51.5
Displacement cc	2991
Valve operation	Twin overhead cams
Ignition	Marelli transistor
Sparkplugs per cyl.	1
Compression ratio	11.5:1
Carburation	Lucas fuel injection
BHP	450 at 10,800 rpm
DRIVE TRAIN	
Clutch	Dry multi-plate
Transmission	5 speed and reverse
Rear axle	Universal jointed halfshafts
CHASSIS	
Frame	Semi monocoque with bulkhead, tubing, riveted aluminium skin
Wheelbase mm	2220
Track – front mm	1425
rear mm	1400
Suspension – front	Upper rocker arms, inboard coil springs and shock absorber units. Wide base lower A arms, anti-roll bar
rear	Single upper links, reversed lower A arms, coil springs and shock absorber units. Long non parallel radius arms, anti-roll bar
Brakes	Lockheed disc
Tyre size – front	5.0/22 × 13
rear	13/26 × 15
Wheels	Campagnolo slotted alloy disc type
Performance (approx)	Max speed 200 mph 0–60 mph 4.7 sec standing quarter mile 11.8 sec

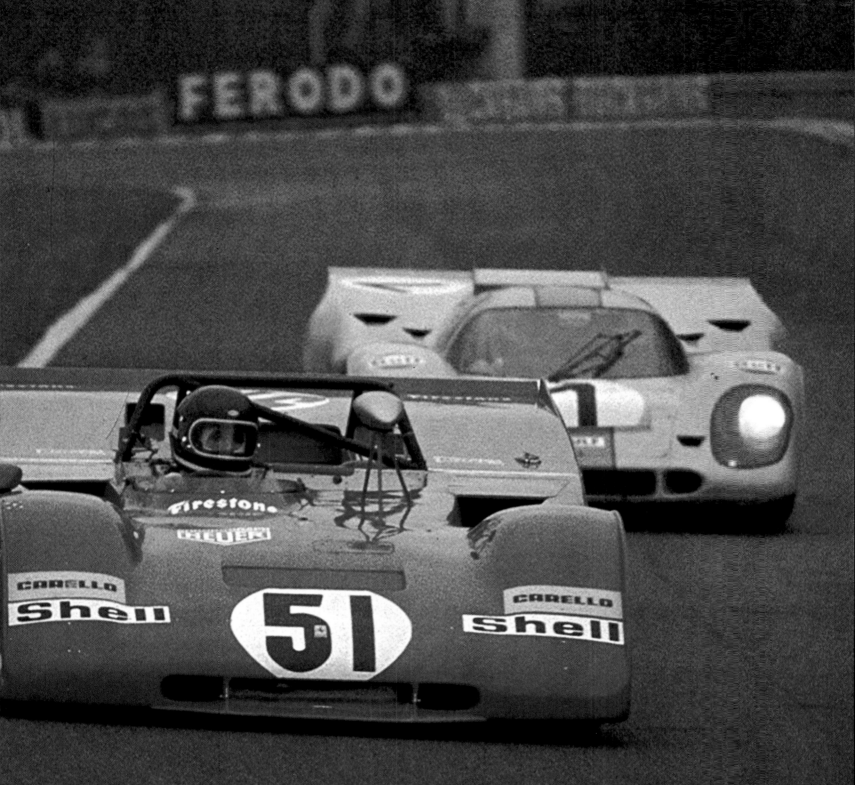

The V12 GT road cars

With the early production machines there are no really clear-cut dividing lines between the grand prix, sports, and gran turismo or berlinetta cars, as all or most were used in competition either by the factory or later by customers, and none could be said to be out-and-out road cars although a number could be used for fast touring. Perhaps the 342 America 2 + 2 Ghia coachwork coupé could be considered as the first attempt, by Ferrari, to introduce a roadgoing automobile. The first of the series (apart from the one displayed at the Brussels show in early 1951) was exhibited at Turin in the spring of that year and was a development of the 340 with the same displacement of 4101 cc but a new chassis and a synchromesh four-speed-and-reverse gearbox, although some featured a five-speed non-synchromesh box. Few were built and they were similar in appearance to the 250 Europa and the later 375 Americas. The chassis, it is interesting to note, was the basis for all the larger Ferraris that came after.

At the 1953 Paris Salon the 250 Europa was introduced and from this period on Ferrari devoted more production time to GT roadgoing cars as these were the forerunners of the 250 series. The Europa had a 2800 mm (9 ft 2 in) wheelbase chassis similar to the 250 MM and also used by the 375 America. There was also the 250 Europa GT which had a shorter wheelbase—2600 mm (8 ft 6 in)—but though both were powered by 3-litre units, the Europa used the Lampredi long-block design engine and the Europa GT the Colombo short-block type. Production of both continued until early 1956, at the latest, with a total number of both types around the mid-50 mark.

March 1956 brought the first appearance, at the Geneva show, of the 250 GT coupé and a subsequent production run of the type until 1960 with nearly 500 cars built. Two versions were on display, one designed and built by Pininfarina and a cabriolet designed and built by Boano. Although it had been intended to market both, the Boano or 'low-roof' cabriolet had a small run of not more than 80 cars. Some of the coupés were designed by Ellena with a 'high roof' but the number produced was minimal. In 1958 Pininfarina designed a new lighter-weight cabriolet for the American market which was built by Scaglietti.

All the 250 GT cars had the 2953 cc V12 engine with a single overhead camshaft per bank of cylinders with bore and stroke of 73 × 58.8 mm, and the early cars had an output of 240 bhp at 7000 rpm and employed three Weber twin-choke carburettors. Some engines had two distributors, others a single unit, and as time progressed the earlier drum brakes were replaced with discs.

Up to the end of 1959 Ferrari had given little thought to the family man but in 1960 he decided to build the 250 GT 2 + 2 (or the 250 GTE as it is also called), the first of the cars being seen at the 1960 Le Mans 24-hour race where it was in use as the course car. True, the cars had two seats at the rear but in practice they could not accommodate two adults. In fact, only young children could sit in any comfort there, for all that the extra space behind the two front seats did was give a larger area for carrying more luggage for protracted holidays. There was an extended production run of the cars for some 900 were built, which proves that Ferrari knew his market.

The normal coupés were dropped from the Ferrari catalogue with the introduction of the 250 GT 2 + 2, but a new berlinetta took their place with a short wheelbase, steel body and more luxurious interior trim, giving greater comfort. The styling was a mixture of the SWB berlinettas and the GTOs and was named the 250 GT Lusso (Lusso meaning luxury) berlinetta or, for short, 250 GTL. The coachwork designed by Pininfarina and built by Scaglietti was aesthetically right with a beautiful line, and it could be said to be the first 'civilized' GT car from the factory, with an interior noise level that did not shatter the eardrums. It could be described as a classic design.

Apart from the closed GT cars Ferrari also produced the 250 GT spyder California in 1958, initially with the short-wheelbase chassis but later models had the longer 2600 mm (8 ft 6 in) chassis.

At the time of the introduction of the long-wheelbase California in Paris in 1961 Ferrari also had a new 2 + 2 on show, and on the Pininfarina stand a one-off Superfast II, an aerodynamic coupé built on the older 4.9-litre 410 Superamerica chassis exhibited at Brussels in 1956. It had a small elliptical grille and the headlamps were retractable; this car was the prototype, if such it can be called, of the 400 Superamericas, which had a short life up to about 1964.

Towards the end of 1963 the factory produced the first version of the 330 GT 2 + 2, a car new in many of its concepts from the earlier GT models. Powered by a V12 4-litre unit based on the original Colombo

ABOVE *Known as the Lusso or luxury car, the 250 GTL has classic lines rarely seen today. Malcolm Clarke's beautiful example of this 1963 car is always a strong concours contender.*

LEFT *Although derided by the press as an ordinary car when it appeared in 1964, the 330 GT 2+2 Mk I was reliable and extremely fast. Owned by K. B. Eckersley, it is a true GT with a 4-litre V12 unit.*

design, it had an output of 300 bhp at 6600 rpm and used a chassis similar in layout to the 250 GT with coil springs and tubular shock absorbers at the front, solid rear axle with semi-elliptic springs and telescopic shock absorbers with concentric coil springs and equipped with four-wheel hydraulic disc brakes. All-round comfort was provided with more headroom and greater accommodation for passengers. Many critics have referred to the car as being dull or ordinary, possibly because its appearance was a trifle nondescript and there were objections to the four-headlamp treatment. The car was certainly different from the more exciting designs of the past, but shape of coachwork does not decide the performance, unless it is totally non-aerodynamic and the 330 was neither a sluggard nor was it unbalanced in any way. However the second or Mark 2 version of 1965 reverted to twin headlamps.

A replacement for the 410 Superamerica made its debut on the Pininfarina stand at the Geneva show in spring 1964; the car was obviously derived from the 410 SA but had a far neater, sleeker line. This was the 500 Superfast with a 4.9-litre V12 unit similar in a number of points to the 330 GT, but the cylinder had pressed-in liners and the head was detachable. There were three Weber 38 DCN carburettors and with an 8.8:1 compression ratio, the engine developed 400 bhp at 6500 rpm. This was a luxury limousine which was faster than other vehicles in its class. Production was limited, the factory turning out one car per month.

Later in 1964 Ferrari brought out two new cars, the 275 GTB and 275 GT spyder, on similar chassis, and for the first time a GT had independent rear suspension. Once again the original Colombo-designed V12 unit was in evidence and it displaced 3.3 litres (bore and stroke of 77 × 53.3mm). The berlinetta's bhp was 280 at 7500 rpm and the spyder's 260 at 7000 rpm, and both had an all-synchromesh five-speed gearbox mounted

at the rear in transaxle form. A new rear suspension developed from racing experience with the 250 LM had parallel 'A' arms with coil springs and a concentric shock absorber, the lower arm being attached to the brake and hub assembly. In shape it owed its lines to the 1964 GTO and 250 LM with a long sloping bonnet, and the headlamps were faired into the wings with plastic covers. A wraparound windscreen, set at a rakish angle, added to the aerodynamic shape and the small rear spoiler provided a touch that denoted its breeding. The usual Borrani wire wheels were discarded for handsome cast-alloy replacements. As an option the factory offered six twin-choke Weber carburettors and a 9.5:1 compression ratio, which increased the bhp to 300. The spyder was a more 'refined' car, a luxury convertible.

Over the next year or so, various modifications were carried out and in 1966 a new double overhead camshaft version of the 3.3-litre engine was installed in the berlinetta chassis and dry-sump lubrication adopted. At the same time the chassis was realigned to overcome problems that had arisen due to misalignment between the engine and transaxle.

Ferrari was still determined to keep the luxury car image alive and introduced in spring 1965 the 4-litre 330 GTC, which was not only superior in finish to his other models but also offered greater interior space and a more powerful engine. In looks it possessed the front aspect of the 500 Superfast and the rear deck of the 330 GT and earned the appellation of being the finest all-round roadgoing Ferrari ever built.

Before leaving the 275 series it should be mentioned that a four-camshaft V12 unit was available late in 1966 producing 300 bhp at 8000 rpm.

As in the earlier years the factory was able to turn out a variety of types either for a series run or for a short run as prototypes for what was to follow. The spring of 1966 saw a 365 California on the stocks but this was abandoned in favour of a new closed type, the 365 GTB/4, giving a choice in 1967 of seven types or variations of types. This must surely have taxed the resources of a not too large concern, even if some of the cars only had a short life.

As was expected, in 1968 the United States regulations on safety and exhaust-emission requirements caused the manufacturers of high-performance cars a number of problems, and especially in Europe where no such legislation was necessary (if indeed it was in America). Maranello fell into line with the 365 GT 2 + 2, a luxury 4.4-litre car with a five-speed transmission in unit with the engine, and independent rear suspension. It was equipped with power steering and air conditioning as standard. Its coachwork followed that of the previous high-class cars turned out by the works, elegant without being in any way outstanding or exciting. It is almost certain that one of the 365 GT 2 + 2s sold in the American market was equipped by its buyer with automatic transmission, using the GM turbo hydraulic system, making it possibly the first Ferrari ever to be thus treated. It was not until the 400 GT, currently in production, that a Ferrari left the factory gates with the choice of either automatic or manual transmission as standard equipment.

While the 365 GTB/4 was not a catalogue-listed type in 1967,

PAGES 66/67 *Between 1964 and 1966, 36 500 Superfasts were designed and built by Pininfarina. The 5-litre V12 unit developed a hefty 400 bhp, and the sweeping lines follow closely those of the 400 Superamerica. This 500 belongs to Ken Bradshaw.*

ABOVE *The 275 GTB/4 was marketed in 1966 and raced by the works and private entrants. James Allington owns this car.*

LEFT *The 275 GTS, a Pininfarina-designed spyder version of the 275 GTB was shown at the 1964 Paris Salon. It produced 260 bhp at 7000 rpm. This is a Concours-winning car and is owned by Alan Eisner.*

RIGHT *Ian Hilton's very desirable 1958 250 GTS California.*

development work for a series run was in progress and testing went ahead during the winter months. Even before it was marketed excitement was mounting regarding its specification and possible general appearance, for it was already being named the Daytona, a name that has stayed with the type ever since. Perhaps some of the many other types manufactured by the factory deserve greater recognition than they received, but the laudatory acclaim heaped on the Daytona was fully justified. There is no doubt that it was, and still is, the ultimate in gran turismo cars, even if the engine was front-mounted when current practice is to have a mid-engined car. It is a car with a charisma, bearing the hallmark of a man who has never accepted second best and it stands as a monument to a living legend in the automobile world.

This 'prima donna' of a car (without, however, the uncertain

LEFT *The elegant 365 GTC/4 was designed and built by Pininfarina and shown at the Paris Salon in 1971. Owned by Lincoln Small.*

BELOW *The legendary 365 GTB/4, restored by David Clarke and owned by JCB Ltd. This type was popularly known as the Daytona.* INSET *Peter Thorpe's 365 GTS which was converted from a berlinetta to a spyder.*

temperament accorded to such humans) was unveiled at the 1968 Paris Salon and won deserved applause without any help from a journalist's road test.

The V12 was a 4.4-litre engine with four overhead camshafts and produced 352 bhp at 7500 rpm. Six 40 DCN 20 Weber carburettors fed the fuel, the compression ratio was 9.3:1, and with a 3.3:1 final drive the maximum speed was 280 km/h (174 mph), probably the highest authentic speed ever attained by a road car. Styling was superb and the design team at Pininfarina had without doubt produced a masterpiece. The low bonnet line had a full-width plastic cover with the lamps set behind, including the indicators, which gave a smooth line from the 'sharp end' to the door panels and pillars, and this line was continued through the rake of the windscreen. The roof line was slim, adding a touch of delicacy, and fell away gradually from the highest point of the screen to the tail which, while it had a cut-off point, was rounded when looked at from the side. The whole effect was one of roundness, of curves without any bulbousness. The slim bumpers were not full-width either in the front or rear but gave maximum cover to the four corners. The interior was, of course in keeping with the purposeful elegance of the kerbside view, with instrumentation nicely balanced and in full view of the driver. The five-

One of the fastest road cars ever built, the 365 GT/BB was not as popular as the Daytona which it superseded in 1973. Capable of over 290 km/h (180 mph), it was in production for three years. This example belongs to Alan Eisner.

spoke knock-off alloy wheels followed Ferrari Formula 1 practice in being straightforward and practical. The bodies were made by Scaglietti who, for once, did not deviate from the original drawings.

In the autumn of 1969 a spyder version was seen at the Frankfurt show, but in the main these cars were built to customer order. Of late a number of Daytona owners have taken their cars to professional coachbuilders to have them converted to the spyder design.

Although the Daytona was not built as a competition car a number of owners and racing équipes have had their cars reworked by the factory so that they could be used in long-distance races such as the Daytona and Le Mans events. Some successes have been achieved but the type will always be remembered as the fastest and probably the best GT car ever built.

By January 1969 the 330 GTC and GTS had been revitalised and, with a single overhead camshaft engine with a capacity of 4390 cc were renamed the 365 GTC and GTS. However, they were phased out at the end of 1970. The following spring, at the Geneva show, Ferrari had on its stand the 365 GTC/4 with a four overhead camshaft engine and a new setting for the six Weber 38 DCOE sidedraft carburettors outside the engine 'V'. Although the bonnet line was low, the front end was squared off and the four headlamps were of the 'pop-up' type. The line from the base of the windscreen to the tail was still flowing but cut off more sharply giving the rear end a sawn-off appearance. This virtually ended the long and exciting run of the V12, except for the current 400 GT front engined limousine.

With the present world fuel shortage it is debatable whether another high-performance Ferrari will appear on the scene when the present range of 12-cylinder road cars have run their course.

Specials and experimental cars

Ferrari has produced something in the order of 300 or more different models since 1946, and this is a staggering figure by any standards. Included in this figure are the experimental types that were tested on the bench, and in some cases also on the track, and were scrapped after design faults or weaknesses had been found. There were also types that never left the design board and were either pigeon-holed or cast into the waste-paper basket. Then there were the specials or one-off designs.

When talking or writing about special or experimental designs one should take pains to understand what precisely is meant by the terms. A 'special' is generally taken to mean a one-off job executed for a specific purpose, such as a certain event or series of events, or for a customer who wants something different from a production car. There have been cars commissioned by such customers that were not specials in the proper sense as they simply used engines no longer required installed in available chassis. A true special is a fairly well-defined car and examples will be given later in the chapter.

There are two views on what constitutes an experimental design. All new designs are experimental up to a point. However, there are those who maintain that a car is experimental even if the designer's brain child, when finally evaluated, is proved to be a viable project before going into production either as a formula car for racing or for a series of roadgoing cars. Others say that the term experimental only applies when the project proves not to be viable after testing and the car is then consigned to an out of the way corner and forgotten.

Let us take an example or two of the first view. The highly successful 500 F2 cars of 2 litres were followed by the 625 F1 2.5-litre, which had an unhappy time when the powers controlling racing decided that Formula 1 races should be contested by cars with the larger-capacity units. The fact that a 625 engine was placed in a 500 chassis, as a test bed, does not constitute an experimental car; it was merely a convenient way of trying out the power unit prior to using a new design of chassis. Nor could the installation of the Dino 156 F1 engine in the semi-monocoque Aero V8 chassis used at Monza in 1963 constitute an experimental design just because the V8 unit was not fully tested in time for the race.

PAGES 74/75 AND THIS PAGE *Tony Vandervell purchased a 375 F1 4.5-litre Ferrari in 1950 which was raced frequently by a number of drivers and was named Thin Wall Special. Over a period of two or three years it was so modified that it scarcely resembled a Ferrari. Note the huge air box between the camboxes. Owned by Vandervell Products.*

A good example of an experimental design resulted from the desire of Rudolf Fischer, a Swiss, to race an F1 car. Ferrari helped out by providing him with one of the swing-axle long-wheelbase chassis from the 1.5-litre supercharged cars and installing a 2.5-litre V12 sports-car unit, designating the car as a 212 F1. He decided to build another installing the same engine in a de Dion chassis used for the 1.5-litre twin-stage blown car. On the data gathered from test-racing the cars, he decided to discard the 2.5-litre engine and using the swing-axle chassis fitted a 3.3-litre unit with bore and stroke of 72 × 68 mm. Only two engines were built; the second powered a sports car, and the racing car was designated a 275 F1. From these trials the 340 F1 emerged and, by enlarging the bore to 80 mm, the capacity was increased to 4.1 litres. A new chassis was built for the car. The 275 F1 was also the basis for the 375 F1, the stroke being lengthened to 74.5 mm to give a capacity of 4493.7 cc. Advancing a further step the 412 M1 was evolved but with a reduction in overall volume to 4023.3 cc.

Ferrari was persuaded to use four of the 375 F1 cars for the 1952 Indianapolis 500 miles, with American drivers, but failed to appreciate the problems involved in chassis and gearbox design for such a race. Being a realist, with other matters on hand, he decided to forget about the project after the cars' abject failure.

On the specials front, Nino Farina decided to have a final crack at the Indy 500-mile event in 1956 and had a 4.4-litre in-line 6 installed in a Kraft Kurtis 500D chassis. Ferrari gave token assistance at the start but decided it was not his type of racing machine and left Farina to further the project; the result again was failure.

The 252 F1 project was a 2-cylinder engine with a bore and stroke of 118 × 114 mm, the long stroke enabling high torque for the more twisty circuits. Capacity was 2493 cc with an output of 175 bhp at 4800 rpm. Although bench-tested the engine was put aside.

Strange as it may appear there were two efforts to mate Ferrari power plants with Cooper chassis. In 1960 the Cooper Castellotti appeared for the Monaco GP, where it failed to qualify, and later retired in the French and Italian races. The engine was the 555 Supersqualo in-line four. The other Cooper had a single overhead camshaft 250 GT engine installed but lacked power. It ran in the 1966 British GP at Brands Hatch, where it finished 11th, and the German event at the Nürburgring, retiring with suspension problems.

In the Tasman series the New Zealander Pat Hoare raced a 1960 Dino 246 F1 chassis powered with a V12 250 Testa Rossa engine. The cubic capacity was 2953 and the output was a respectable 300 bhp, but it was not a great success, being outpaced by the faster Coopers and Lotuses.

A highly successful special, designated 212E, was campaigned by Peter

Schetty for the European Hill Climb Championship in 1969. It had a 2-litre flat-12 engine developed from the grand prix boxer unit. Bore and stroke was 65 × 50 mm with a compression ratio of 11:1 and output was 280 bhp. It made all the other cars in the championship look like hacks!

Among the special cars built for a specific purpose should be included those that were contenders for the earlier CanAm races instituted in 1966 as a championship for Group 7 cars. The NART organization under Luigi Chinetti entered the first Ferrari for the 1967 series, having sent a P3/4 to Modena for updating and body modifications. However, the car was some five seconds down per lap compared with the McLarens. Each year the story was repeated until Enzo decided that, with all his other commitments, there was insufficient time to modify the cars and he therefore left their competition preparation in the hands of owners.

Mention should be made of the 'Thinwall Specials' owned by Tony Vandervell, the man who later went on to produce the Vanwall GP car. The Vandervell organization, having sold the idea of using 'Thinwall' bearings to Ferrari, managed to acquire a 1.5-litre single-stage blown grand prix car from the factory. It was a disastrous purchase: a brute to handle even in a straight line, it was finally crashed. The second car with twin cams per bank and twin-stage supercharging was not to Tony Vandervell's liking and was soon returned to the works and exchanged for a 4.5-litre 1950 car. This gave complete satisfaction and the Vandervell works carried out many modifications so that in the end it bore scant resemblance to a Ferrari.

A number of body-design exercises have appeared from time to time that obviously could not be classified as one-off specials, or even experimental cars, since the coachwork clothed existing chassis with production engines. In 1969 Pininfarina produced an outstanding design for the 512S which was shown at Turin. The only problem was the rear-view visibility, which was virtually nil. The following year Pininfarina came out with another 'visionary' design using the 512S chassis as the basis, but no engine was installed. The one problem with the project was that the car could have been driven only in a straight line as the all-enveloping body did not allow for any movement of the front wheels!

ABOVE LEFT *In the 1966 British and German GPs, Chris Lawrence drove the Cooper chassis car with a Ferrari 250 GT engine installed. He retired at the Nürburgring.*

LEFT *Richard Phillips imported this car from South Africa and it is probably the only 225 S with this style of chassis in the world. Built for Count Marzotto, it won the 1952 Mille Miglia.*

ABOVE *Another version of the 1952 225 S; this is the short-chassis spyder model.*

RIGHT *The 375 F1 was not a wholly successful car and examples were sold to private individuals. This well-restored 1952 example was probably the prototype for the Indianapolis racers. It now belongs to Gavin Bain of New Zealand.*

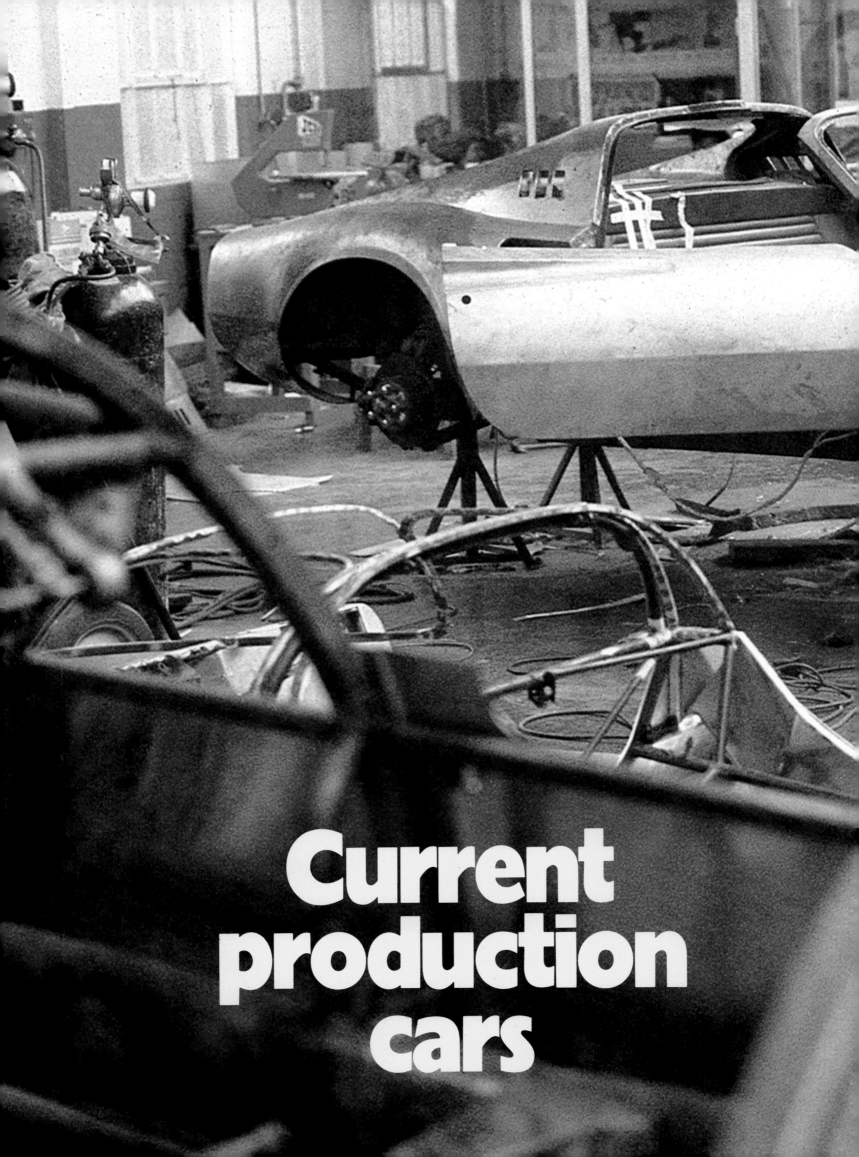

Current
production
cars

For high-class performance cars the present production range from the Ferrari factory offers customers a wide choice. Admittedly the buyer is a person of discernment who appreciates quality engineering coupled with an aesthetic taste for superb styling, and finally the cash to buy such a car. Some might feel the prices are rather high, but a glance at the quality automobile market of today shows there is little, or no, difference between a Ferrari and a number of other marques.

The present range consists of two V8s, the 308 GT4 2 + 2 and 308 GTB (including a spyder model, the 308 GTS), both mid-engined cars; the 400 GT front-engined V12 with either automatic or manual transmission; and finally the 512 berlinetta boxer with the flat-12 mid-mounted unit.

Although Ferrari made the 250 series over a long period, it could not be said that they were a production range in the true sense since there were a number of variants, and even in the variants it can be said that there were differences. As an example there is no guarantee that the valve sizes on the 250 short-wheelbase cars were always the same and this also applied to the long-wheelbase models and others in the range, and such differences were not confined to valves alone.

It was not until 1968 when the Daytona, or 365 GTB/4 to give it the correct designation, first appeared at the Paris show that Ferrari started what could be termed a real production run. A year later the Dino 246 GT, a 2.4-litre V6 two-seater, made its debut at the Paris show and was to set a pattern for many years to come, not only for Ferraris but for other aspiring constructors as well, in having an engine placed behind the driving compartment on a roadgoing car. It also set a standard of styling that was the envy of its competitors and which they have not been able to emulate. Its simple, sleek, flowing lines have never been equalled; it was a jewel to gaze upon and bore out the old adage that what looks right must be right. Before its demise in 1974 a spyder version was marketed and proved even more popular than the GT model. These cars were conceived and designed by the master coachbuilder Pininfarina, although they were built by Scaglietti.

PAGES 80/81 *The workshop at Maranello Concessionaires, Thorpe, UK.*

RIGHT *The 308 GTS was introduced in 1977 and, with traditional Pininfarina lines, found immediate popularity. Owned by J. L. Barder.*

BELOW *The family man's car, the 308 GT4 2+2, which was introduced in 1973. This example is owned by Australian Greg Norman.*

To replace the Dino 246 Ferrari unveiled his next production, the Dino 308 GT4 2 + 2, at the 1973 Paris show. Although the styling was pleasant, the original production models did not have quite the same aesthetic appeal as their predecessor. This could be accounted for by the fact that Ferrari had the coachwork styled by Bertone, a company not noted for giving a 'roundness' to its designs although, when not attempting a compromise design, it does produce some 'no nonsense' and pleasing styles. With the 308 GT Bertone did have the added problem of designing a 2 + 2 car, which does not allow for a flowing line at the rear, especially when the engine is rear-mounted.

The chassis and suspension followed the well-tried pattern of the 246, which had given outstanding handling characteristics, and the only change was to increase the track to give a greater body width. Fore and aft suspension consisted of upper and lower wishbones, coil springing, telescopic dampers and anti-roll bars. The 90-degree V8 engine was set transversely behind the centre line and had twin overhead camshafts per bank of cylinders. To keep a low profile at the rear the five-speed all-synchromesh-and-reverse gearbox was placed at the rear of the engine and not beneath it. A helical spur-type final drive with limited-slip differential drove the rear wheels through solid shafts. With a bore of 81 mm and stroke of 71 mm the total displacement was 2927 cc and the output 250 bhp at 7700 rpm. The Campagnolo light-alloy wheels were attractive and shod with Michelin 205/70 VR 14 XWX steel-braced radial tyres. The pop-up twin headlamps permitted a smooth-sloping frontal contour.

Since the early days the line of the 308 GT has been improved and now looks like the thoroughbred it is. With a maximum and genuine top speed of 246 km/h (154 mph) it is undoubtedly the car for the family man with no more than two small children who can indulge his passion for a high-performance car with superb all-round visibility seldom met in the more exotic car market, provided he has the purchase price. On top of all that he can point to the fact that the Dino 308 GT4 changed its image in 1976 when it was officially designated a Ferrari and given the famous prancing horse as its badge.

Whatever the 308 GT4 2 + 2 lacked in aesthetic appeal, the next offering from the factory was awaited with impatience, for the rumours and some sneak preview pictures indicated a car that was going to be received with enthusiasm. As so often with new models from Maranello, the 308 GTB, as it was called, made its appearance at the Paris show, in 1975. Unlike all previous cars of the marque, it had a glass fibre body. Ferrari had, very wisely, gone back to the artistry of Pininfarina to design the body line, and what a superb job that concern made of it: in a style that combined the best from the 246 GT and the 365 berlinetta boxer to create something new that it would be very difficult for other coachwork designers to emulate for other high-class cars. Scaglietti built the bodies and it was extremely difficult to tell whether steel or some other material had been used, so superb was the finish.

The body is long and with a low roofline has the look of a dart, with an unobtrusive spoiler below the nose and the hint of a spoiler on the tail end of the engine lid. From nose to roofline there is scarcely a break and the sail planes from the back end of the roof continue the unobtrusive, sleek line. The maximum height of the car is only 1168 mm (3 ft 10 in), which might suggest that there is little headroom, but the rake of the well-designed seats ensures that even a person of more than average height need have no fear of his or her head rubbing the lining. Although the cockpit might appear cramped for two people, it is in fact larger than it looks and there is even room behind the seats to stuff any number of medium-sized parcels and other odds and ends, and in addition there is a baggage compartment between the engine and tail where large suitcases can be stowed.

The 3-litre 90-degree V8 engine has twin overhead camshafts per bank of cylinders, and though similar in many respects to the 308 GT4 units there are essential differences. The engine is placed transversely behind the seating compartment and about amidships with the drive taken from the left end, via the clutch, to a set of drop gears, which reverse the drive from left to right and then back to left to right to the five-speed all-synchromesh-and-reverse gearbox. The final drive has a limited-slip differential. Dry-sump oil lubrication is a feature and the reasons for employing this method are many: they include additional cooling area, the halting of oil surge and a reduction in engine height—apart from the fact that the system allows for further development of the unit should the constructor have racing in mind, always a possibility with Ferrari.

Although the chassis and suspension follow the general pattern of the sister car, the anti-roll bars fore and aft are strengthened to limit the

PAGES 84/85 *To compete with other manufacturers in the luxury-car market, Ferrari brought out the 400 GT in 1976, with automatic and manual transmission. This superb four-seater can now be bought with fuel induction. The driver's compartment* (INSET) *features a well-designed console and neatly grouped instruments.*

ABOVE *The current boxer, designated 512 BB, replaced the 365 GT/BB in 1976. Flowing lines give the car (owned by L. Page) a purposeful look.*

amount of suspension travel in such a low car and the wheelbase is some 221 mm (8.7 in) shorter. The harder suspension, reminiscent of many early sports cars, gives a ride at low speed that 'feels' all the indentations unfortunately found on most roads today except motorways. As speed is increased so the ride becomes more comfortable.

Both the 308s have electrically operated windows and rear windscreen heaters, and the instrumentation is well grouped, clear and without fuss. The main optional extra is air conditioning, and on the 308 GTB wide-rim wheels are available, but these are equipped with the normal Michelin 205/70 VR12 radial-ply tubeless tyres; both the standard and wide-rim wheels have the now familiar attractive light-alloy five-spoke design. Although the configuration of the GTB gives the impression that it could easily outpace the GT4, the fact remains that its top speed is also 246 km/h (154 mph) and its behaviour on the road is not quite up to the standard of the 2 + 2 cars, especially under adverse weather conditions but this, of course, does depend on the travelling speed.

In mid-1977 it was decided to abandon glass fibre for the coachwork and revert to steel.

In Italy a smaller-engined car, the 208 GT4, was produced and sold for a time; the idea was fuel economy, that country suffering shortages even before they had become general. One such car was imported into the

United Kingdom, but the engine was removed and replaced by the normal 3-litre unit.

Ferrari—or should it be Fiat?—was quite late in entering the quality-limousine market, for it was not until the Paris show in 1976 that his first such offering was on view. There can be little doubt that the factory had been missing out on a growing trend—a top car for the top executive—and this was being met by a number of manufacturers, although few of the cars could carry a prestige label. Ferrari reverted, once more, to the familiar V12 front-engined car that had served the factory so well over many years. Labelled the 400 GT, it may be bought with either automatic or manual transmission. The manual operation is through a five-speed synchromesh-and-reverse gearbox. The model is a full four-seater luxury car with power-assisted steering and air conditioning as standard equipment. The coachwork, styled by Pininfarina and also built by the firm, is pleasant to look at but has nothing outstanding that would make a passer-by stand and stare. It follows in the footsteps of the 365 GT4 2 + 2, which was marketed between 1972 and 1976.

For town driving where traffic is comparatively dense a car with automatic transmission appeals, not only to the more elderly, but also to many younger drivers as it takes the strain of finding a lower gear when a gearshift has to be manipulated.

The V12 unit has a bore and stroke of 81 × 78 mm giving a capacity of 4823 cc and a robust power output of 340 bhp at 6500 rpm. There are twin overhead camshafts per bank of cylinders and the electrics are fired by twin distributors. Six twin-choke sidedraft 38 DCOE 59/60 Weber carburettors feed the fuel. Suspension, as with all modern Ferraris, is fully independent fore and aft.

At the same Paris show in 1976 where the 400 GT was on display, Ferrari introduced the second version of his berlinetta boxer, the 512 BB, as he phased out the earlier model, which had been in production for

three years. The newer type retains the horizontally opposed (boxer) 12-cylinder engine rear-mounted, but the capacity has been increased by 552 cc to 4942 cc by lengthening the stroke from 71 to 78 mm and increasing the bore from 81 to 82 mm. The usual twin overhead camshafts per bank of cylinders are in evidence and electronic ignition and a single distributor fire the plugs. The lubrication is dry sump and the fuel is fed via four triple-choke downdraft Weber 40 IF3C carburettors. Suspension is independent all round and the gearbox, mounted similarly to that of the 308 GTB, has five forward speeds and a reverse.

The styling is quite similar to that of the 308 GTB, with sleek flowing lines, a spoiler at the sharp end, and again the hint of an uplift at the tail. The body in fact differs only in some detail from the earlier model. From whichever angle it is viewed it exudes a brutish and extremely powerful presence, but for all that has an elegance befitting a Pininfarina creation.

What of the future? Will Ferrari's presence still be felt in engine design? Will a new front-engined V12 with sporting characteristics come from the factory, or will the purely financial considerations of the mighty Fiat empire take complete control and sweep away all that Enzo has built up in his good and bad years? Dare Fiat erase the magic and aura of the name Ferrari, which stands for excellence and reliability? It is hard to believe the company would contemplate such a drastic step, for the Italians know that craftsmanship in engineering and design count for more than almost anything else, even if the robot takes over from man's hands on the production line.

Rumour says that another version of the 512 BB will be marketed in either 1980 or 1981 but it is difficult to see how an extension of this 'line' could make any impact on the public. Perhaps a completely restyling exercise embodying the best from the Modulo (the coachwork exercise by Pininfarina) would go a long way to making the adrenalin flow freely once more.

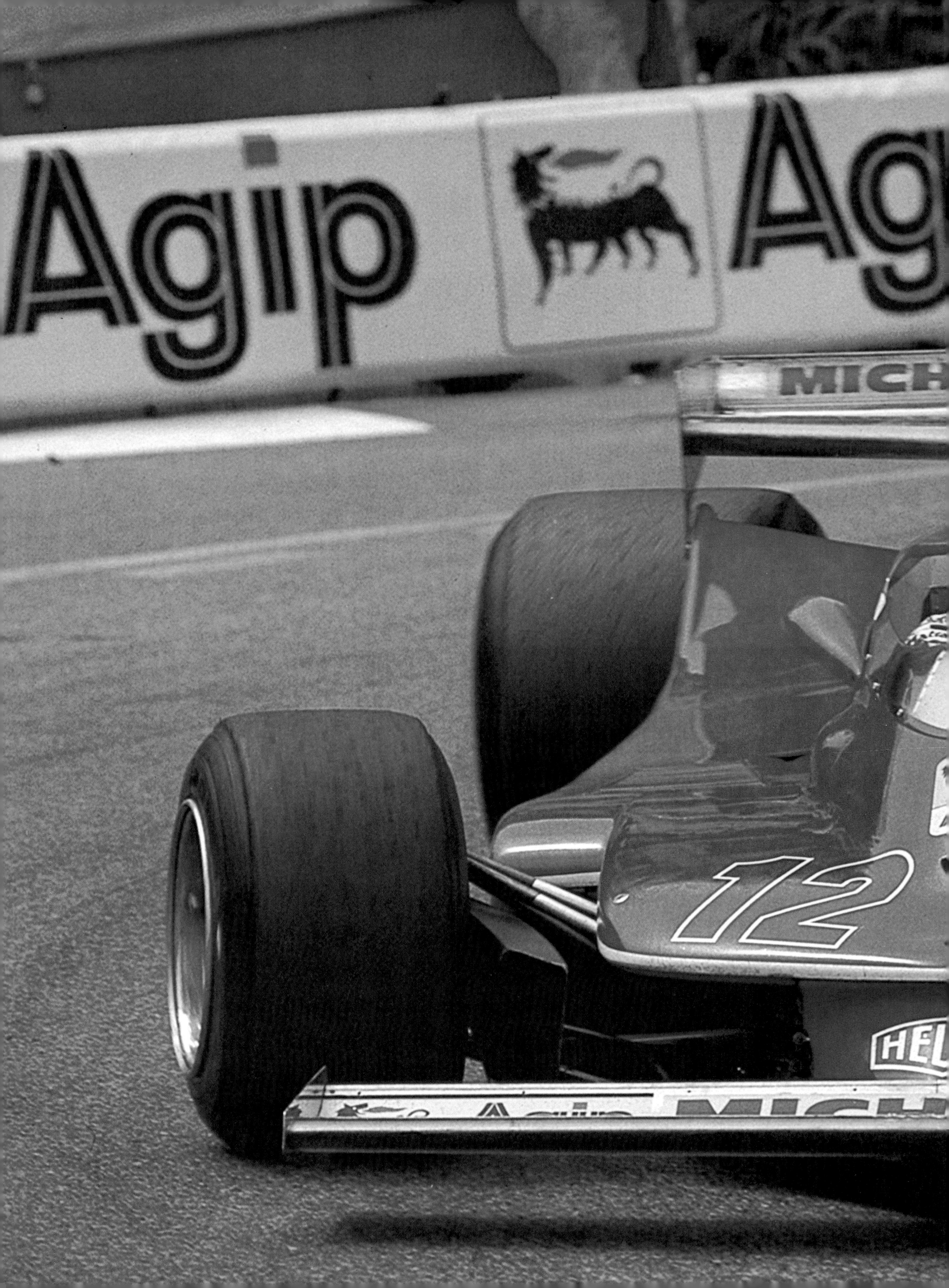
Agip
12

The racing drivers

For 33 years Enzo Ferrari has been racing cars bearing his name in grand prix, sports-racing and gran turismo events and so he has obviously engaged a multitude of drivers during these three decades. To do justice to the drivers, at least the more prominent of them, would need a separate book, so this account must concentrate on those who have gained worldwide fame.

It has been noted already that, over the years, a great deal of acrimony has arisen between Ferrari and the national press of Italy, and much of this stems from the fact that the more emotional motoring journalists have felt that Italian drivers have been overlooked and those of other nationalities favoured. This is not altogether true for the record says that at least 21 Italians have been behind the wheel of the Ferrari grand prix cars and there were many more who drove the sports-racing and gran turismo cars in races. Against this figure around 60 drivers from other countries have been engaged to drive the Formula 1 cars, but from this number some only had a drive or two and there were a few who were contracted to drive in other events.

Of the Italians, Lorenzo Bandini held a contract for six years from 1962 before he was killed, and Alberto Ascari and the German Wolfgang von Trips each drove for Ferrari for six years before they too died as a result of crashes. In numbers British drivers take second place to the Italians with no fewer than eight having contracts, although one or two were short term. Peter Collins, Mike Hawthorn, John Surtees and Mike Parkes are names of British drivers who come readily to people's minds.

Ferrari's first three drivers were Giuseppe 'Nino' Farina, Raymond Sommer, nicknamed the Boar of the Ardennes, and Prince Bira who made his name in the 1930s as a superb driver of voiturettes with ERAs.

As many of the more recent drivers are well known to present-day motor racing enthusiasts perhaps it is fitting to recall, in some detail, the men who drove Ferraris in the early days.

Alberto Ascari was the son of the famous Italian driver Antonio Ascari who was a leading member of the Alfa Romeo team and who, on occasions, had raced with Enzo Ferrari in the same team. Antonio met his death when leading in the 1925 French GP on the Montlhéry Autodrome. He was then 37: Alberto was killed at the same age when testing a sports Ferrari for a friend at Monza four days after being involved in an accident at Monte Carlo when driving the Lancia D50.

Ascari was a burly, well-built young man who would have had some difficulty in fitting himself into the cockpit of a current Formula 1 car. As with many Italian drivers he came to four wheels after racing motorcycles, where his early successes brought him a contract to ride in the Bianchi team in 1937. His first efforts on four wheels, in 1940, were unsuccessful, and then World War 2 overtook motor racing and Alberto took to the mountains as he had no stomach for fighting on the same side as the Germans. After the hostilities, with the help and encouragement of his friend and mentor Luigi Villoresi, a well-established pre-war racing driver, he started his career in 1947 as a guest driver for Piero Taruffi, who had been asked to put on a demonstration race at Cairo; the car was a Fiat-based Cisitalia and Ascari came in second. During the same year on the Modena circuit and driving a Maserati he won his first race.

From 1947 Ascari started his climb to the top, although the going at first was hard, but his sheer enthusiasm for the sport and readiness to drive anything brought his name to the attention of the people who mattered. By 1948, when he was getting more rides, his career took an upward turn, for, after several first places in Italian events, he was second behind Villoresi in the RAC GP at Silverstone driving the 4CLT/48 Maserati.

Ferrari had obviously been watching the 30-year-old driver. He signed him on for the 1949 season and at the same time secured Villoresi's signature. In all, Ascari secured five first places in a variety of races, some of significance such as the Swiss GP and the all-important Italian GP, and others minor events. In many races he made fastest lap, following Villoresi's advice that the man who gets out in front can then dictate the race and frequently wins. The demise of the 125 F1 cars came in 1950 as Ferrari had decided on a larger-capacity engine and introduced the Lampredi-designed 3.3-, 4.1- and 4.5-litre units. Ascari took full advantage of the change by winning seven races in the year and six more in 1951.

In 1952 the premier races were contested by the 2-litre Formula 2 cars; Ferrari ran his 500 F2 cars and Ascari showed his undoubted prowess by winning 13 events and becoming world champion driver—his 6 victories the following year gave him his second championship. At the end of the 1953 season he and Ferrari could not agree terms so Ascari left to drive the Lancia D50 cars. However, 1954 was a frustrating year as these cars had not been fully developed by Vittorio Jano. Ascari therefore picked up drives where he could, but mainly in sports-racing events—even driving for Ferrari.

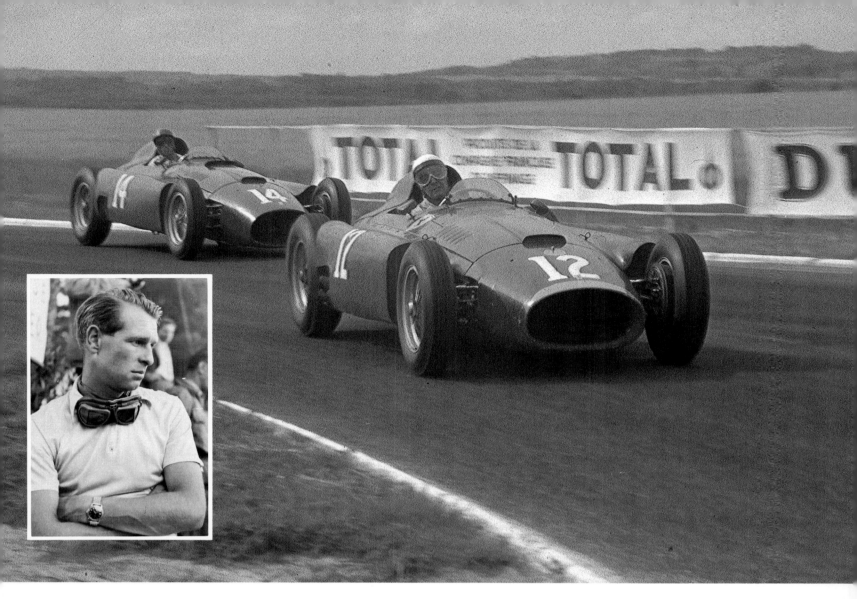

PAGES 88/89 *Gilles Villeneuve with the 312 T4 at the 1979 Monaco GP.*

LEFT *Alberto Ascari on his way to victory in a 500 F2, 1953 British GP.*

ABOVE *Eugenio Castellotti leads Peter Collins in the 1956 French GP at Rheims, both driving Lancia-Ferraris.* INSET *Peter Collins in pensive mood.*

By 1955 the Lancia D50 was raceworthy and before his accident in the Monte Carlo race and death four days later, he had won the Naples and Turin GPs in the new car.

Alberto Ascari was undoubtedly one of the best racing drivers in the world, with a 'press-on' mentality that paid off; his death left a great void for he was an exuberant and happy type.

Peter Collins began his racing career on four wheels—but powered by a 500 cc JAP motorcycle engine, a form of motor racing pioneered by the British after World War 2 for those who wanted to enter the sport but whose funds were limited.

Like his great friend, Mike Hawthorn, Collins was a true professional but was in big-time racing because he loved the sport and not for what he could get out of it financially. His first drives came in 1952 when he joined the HWM team with Lance Macklin and Stirling Moss. From this point on he drove a great variety of cars in many types of races, gaining invaluable experience, and it was not until 1956 that he was invited to sign a contract to drive for Scuderia Ferrari.

It was the year when Enzo Ferrari was at the crossroads for he really had nothing in his team until the Lancia concern handed him all its D50 machines and equipment. So Collins's first taste of motor racing for the Scuderia was with an 'alien' car, but he made full use of his opportunity and by the end of the season found himself third in the world drivers' championship, only a few points behind Fangio and Moss. During his first season with the Scuderia he had the maestro Fangio as team leader and was careful to study his driving technique. This paid off as Fangio was certainly impressed by Collins's approach to motor racing and was heard to remark that he considered both Collins and Hawthorn would become

future world champions: high praise indeed. Fangio's praise was not without reason for in his first season Collins won two grands prix: the Belgian race on 3 June at the fast Spa Francorchamps circuit; and the ACF GP at Rheims on 1 July from Castellotti by 0.3 second.

On a number of occasions in the early days Collins had to give up his car, when in a favourable position, to allow a senior member of the team to take over because his car was failing. In the main he took this philosophically, being essentially a team man, but at times he felt more than a little angry. However, during the 1956 Italian GP at Monza he made the grand gesture himself so that Fangio could win the world drivers' title, for if the great man had scored no points in the race he would have lost the championship. Collins knew that Fangio's Ferrari was very sick and was eventually forced to retire, so he also went into the pits, got out of his car and told Fangio to take over. Fangio was astounded at this sporting gesture and, after having to make up some 25 seconds with a lap to go, he was second across the line 5.7 seconds behind Moss and kept the title by three points.

For Ferrari 1957 was a poor year and during the season Collins collected a meagre 8½ championship points. But it was not all disappointment, for he had quite a good season driving the sports-racing cars even if he did not win an important event. As long as he was racing he was happy.

For 1958 the factory had the Dino 246 ready, another Ferrari and not a makeshift like the Lancia-Ferrari, and the drivers were hoping for better things. Indeed it was a better season, but the end was near for Peter Collins after he had won the British GP at Silverstone on 19 July. The German event was run, as usual, at the Nürburgring and both Mike Hawthorn and Peter Collins 'played' with the opposition until Tony Brooks in the Vanwall came into their mirrors and the race was really on. Three cars were nose to tail and on lap 11, Hawthorn expected Collins to pass him on the long return straight. But he took Hawthorn on the fast curve at Pflanzgarten and, going too fast, ran wide and hit the outside bank, the car rearing into the air. Peter Collins was flown to Bonn but it was too late. So died a cavalier of motor racing, a professional sportsman mourned by all who love the sport.

Giuseppe Farina, or 'Nino' to his friends, was a complex man who could be either remote or friendly: although reasonably fluent in English he would at times pretend he had no knowledge of the language. He was a Doctor of Law but was persuaded by his rich merchant friend Gino Rovere to take up motor racing in 1933 and continued until 1955 when he retired. His father was the famous Italian coachbuilder who later joined his uncle to found the Pininfarina firm.

Nino was a superb athlete, handsome and with a good physique. Unlike many racing drivers he had a feeling and sympathy for things mechanical and Ferrari described him as the 'complete driver', for he not only drove many types of racing cars but was at home in any kind of event. It could be said that he modelled his driving technique on that of Nuvolari, as they both competed at the same time. Fear was not in his make up and he kept his foot on the 'loud' pedal until the last moment, sometimes escaping injury but occasionally doing damage to himself and others. Some would describe him as ruthless, others felt he had a fiery determination.

He joined Scuderia Ferrari in 1936 and found himself among the great drivers of the day, but this did not deter him from expressing himself.

After World War 2 Farina rejoined Alfa Romeo and when that team was 'resting' went over to Maseratis and also freelanced, but drove a 2-litre Ferrari in the Argentinian Formule Libre races in 1949. He was back with the Alfa team in 1950, winning race after race and taking the newly constituted world drivers' championship. However, 1951 was his final year with the team as the factory withdrew the cars from racing.

In 1952 he joined Ferrari who already had a star in Ascari. Farina found that he literally had to take second or third place to his brilliant team mate who became world champion driver in 1952 and 1953. The new 2.5-litre Formula 1 for 1954 did not enhance Farina's reputation as the 625 F1 cars lacked power, and apart from that he was involved in two serious incidents: in the Mille Miglia he crashed, damaging an arm and being badly bruised; and a halfshaft sheared in the Monza 1000 km race, holing the fuel tank with the result that the car caught fire, causing him serious burns which put him out of racing for some time. In 1955 he decided to retire. Then in 1966, on his way to a race meeting at Rheims, he was killed when he took a curve too fast and left the road before crashing.

Mike Hawthorn, like Peter Collins, treated motor racing as a sporting venture. His father was a garage proprietor in Surrey, so Mike had been brought up with cars and soon found himself involved in racing at club level and then gradually made his way to a higher grade by harrying all and sundry with his very fast Cooper Bristol.

By 1952 Hawthorn had been earmarked by Ferrari and in 1953 he signed to drive the red cars. Ferrari already had a strong hand for the season with Ascari (1952 champion), 'Nino' Farina (1950 champion) and veteran Villoresi, but he decided to add 24-year-old Hawthorn. It was not expected that Hawthorn would outshine any of his team mates, but he was always the solid back-up man and rarely was he out of the money. Perhaps his greatest race, indeed it was one of the most memorable races ever, was the ACF GP run over the fast Rheims circuit. Here, Mike Hawthorn ran wheel to wheel against Fangio over the last 250 km (150 miles), passing and repassing each other until finally Hawthorn came out of Fangio's slipstream to take the chequered flag by a car's length. Gonzalez was third and Farina fourth with 4.6 seconds separating the four cars.

As the new boy Hawthorn had enjoyed his first season; even if he failed to win another major event he had at least upheld Ferrari prestige.

In early April 1954 Hawthorn crashed at Syracuse, the car burst into flames and he was in hospital with severe burns until June. It was a wretched year, for the new 625 F1 2.5-litre cars were not really competitive and despite the numerous modifications were never on full song. Mike's father was killed in a road accident and his mother was in poor health, and then having to look after the garage business did not improve his morale. For 1955 he had contracts with Tony Vandervell,

Jaguar and Ferrari, the latter two for sports-car racing, but his patch of bad luck was still running for in the Le Mans 24-hour race he convinced himself that he was the cause of the horrendous accident involving Pierre Levegh (Mercedes) and numerous spectators Mike Hawthorn was exonerated at the enquiry and blame for the accident was ascribed to no one. He returned to Ferrari for the Italian GP but had to retire.

The 1956 season was little better and it was not until 1958 that he came into his own once more and, although he won the drivers' world championship, it was through his consistent driving and not by winning grands prix that he amassed a total of 42 points. At the season's end he retired from the sport, but sadly did not live long enough to settle down and enjoy a normal life for a car he was driving on the Guildford bypass skidded and, crashing into a tree, Mike died.

Stirling Moss was much admired by Enzo Ferrari as far back as the early 1950s when the John Heath and George Abecassis team of HWMs were harrying the Ferraris and Moss was the man most feared by the drivers of the red cars.

Ferrari sent a telegram to Moss inviting him to drive one of his cars in both the 1951 British and French GPs. However, Moss had a commitment to drive an HWM in a Formula 2 event at Avus on the same day as the French race, but agreed to join the Scuderia for the British GP. However, Ferrari decided against letting Moss drive in only the British event.

Nevertheless Ferrari invited Moss to Modena and signed him to drive the prototype 2.5-litre 625 car at Bari on September 2. Arriving at Bari, Moss was informed that his seat had been given to Piero Taruffi. To ease Moss' annoyance David Murray offered to share his F2 Ferrari in the race but the car, which had been raced by Peter Whitehead in F1 events, was old and during practice Moss rammed some bales having 'run out' of brakes. Although the car was repaired it was retired before he could have a chance to drive.

During the next few years Ferrari made various overtures to Moss but he had decided not to drive for the Scuderia after his earlier treatment. December 1957 saw Moss at the Bahamas Speedweek (also known as the cocktail party races') with an Aston Martin DBR3/370 and after two events the car was loaned to a lady to drive. She promptly turned it over, but luck was with him for both Temple Bluell and Jan de Vroom each had a 290 MM Ferrari entered and offered their cars to him. Choosing

Vroom's car he won his race by a handsome margin from Carroll Shelby's 450 S Maserati, following this up in February 1958 with a victory in Havana, driving a 3.8-litre Tipo 315.

It was not until 1960 that Moss found himself behind the wheel of a Ferrari once more. Rob Walker and Dick Wilkins entered a brand-new 250 short-wheelbase Ferrari for him for the revived Tourist Trophy event at Goodwood, which he won by two laps, and a week later he won the Redex Trophy race at Brands Hatch in the same car. In the November the car was shipped to Nassau for a Tourist Trophy event and victory came his way for the third time. The Walker/Wilkins combination bought another 250 swb (having sold the original one) and entered it in the 1961 Le Mans race under the North American Racing Team banner with Moss sharing the car with Graham Hill. It ran steadily in fourth position for nine hours when the oil pressure began falling. The car was out of the race a few laps later when the radiator hose split and, despite a replacement, the damage had been done to the engine. Moss drove the same car in three further races, winning on each occasion. He again drove for NART at Daytona in February 1962, finishing fourth in the GT class in a special Pininfarina-bodied car on a 250 swb chassis. At Sebring on 23 March he shared a TRI/61 Ferrari with Innes Ireland but the car was disqualified when Ireland took the car into the pits for brake adjustments and a mechanic topped up with fuel before the permitted time.

A few weeks later Moss called on Enzo Ferrari at Modena where they patched up their previous differences and Stirling came away with a promise of a drive in a new 156 F1, which would be maintained by the works. Even more surprising it was agreed that the car would be painted in the blue of the Rob Walker Équipe. But before this happened Moss had a terrible accident, which ended his racing career but luckily not his life.

Peter Neild Whitehead was a British driver who deserves more than a casual mention as he was one of the great amateurs who made a name for himself driving the early Ferraris. Whitehead was a farmer and had been racing before World War 2; he can only be described as the true 'gentleman driver' of postwar international racing.

From 1949 he was involved for nine years with the Ferrari factory. The first car he bought, at a time when Ferrari grand prix cars were for sale, was the 125 F1 1.5-litre V12 model, and although he was taken under the wing of the prancing horse Scuderia, he retained his amateur status.

Perhaps Whitehead will be remembered best for his heroic efforts to win the 1949 Grand Prix de France at Rheims, a race full of drama. Towards the end of the event, when a number of contestants had dropped out for one reason or another, two cars were battling for the lead and the honours: they were veteran Louis Chiron driving the large 4.5-litre Lago Talbot and Peter Whitehead in the diminutive 1.5-litre Ferrari—painted green, this being the British international colour. In the closing stages Peter had managed to get ahead and was drawing away steadily. With 174 km (108 miles) to go the thirsty V12 blown Ferrari had to refuel, but Whitehead was determined to win and after 11 laps regained the lead. On lap 57 with 7 to go, the gearbox drain plug fell out and the gear selectors jammed leaving him with fourth gear only. Louis Chiron won and Prince Bira took second place with Whitehead, the hero of both the crowd and press, third. He did, however, have the satisfaction of making the fastest lap, and two months later won the Czech GP.

For a minor race in Jersey in 1949 Whitehead was nominated as the Ferrari entrant and during the season he joined the team when required. In all he took part in ten races during the year, finishing in seven.

From 1950 onwards he freelanced again, won the Jersey road race and Ulster Trophy in a Ferrari and also raced in Europe, Australasia, Argentina and South Africa: sometimes in Ferraris, and now and again in Jaguars and Aston Martins in sports-car events. In Australasia he upheld the marque by winning and being placed in a number of races.

Entered with his brother Graham in the 1958 Tour de France, a long-distance race where competitive events were linked with long tours on the highways, Peter crashed badly on a road section and was sadly killed.

BELOW *Between 1962 and 1967 Lorenzo Bandini was a staunch member of the Ferrari team. Apart from driving formula racing cars he adapted himself to long-distance events, including the Targa Florio.*

INSET TOP LEFT *Peter Whitehead, the English farmer who so nearly won the 1949 French GP in his private 125 F1.*

INSET BOTTOM LEFT *Niki Lauda, a great and dedicated driver who also excelled as a tester. His contribution to Ferrari was in winning two world drivers' championships.*

INSET BOTTOM RIGHT *In his first season with Ferrari (1979) Jody Scheckter became World Champion. He is seen here with the 1980 312 T5.*

Of course there were many more drivers of diverse nationalities and talents who should be allotted more than a line or two. Some may think that the Argentinian, Juan Manuel Fangio, should receive more than a passing mention since many people consider him to be the best driver to have sat behind the wheel of a racing car, but he signed for Ferrari for one season only. Although he won one of his five world drivers' championships in the Lancia-Ferraris in 1956 it does seem as though he was not a happy member of the team; he felt that Enzo Ferrari never gave him the best car to drive so he left at the end of the season.

Although the other Argentinian, Froilan Gonzalez, appeared to flit in and out of the Scuderia, presumably of his own accord, in all he had contracts covering a period of five years between 1951 and 1960. Gonzalez was a man who seemed to have no fear, but on the other hand he was not ruthless and showed consideration to others in a race.

Giancarlo Baghetti was one of those stars who now and again come on the scene and after competing in minor events in a variety of cars, arrive in a big way to startle all the established names. This he did in 1961. However, his descent was just as rapid the following year, but perhaps this was due more to the quality of the Ferrari than his skill as a driver.

Of the other Italians, Luigi Villoresi was an early member of the

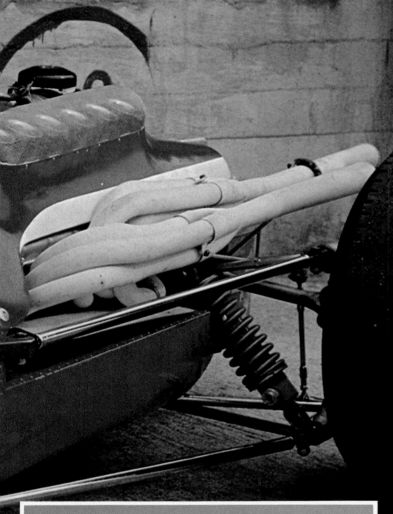

Scuderia—but he was nearing the end of a long and distinguished career as a driver. Luigi Musso and Eugenio Castolletti, on the other hand, were taken on during the mid-1950s. The former was somewhat wild in his approach to motor racing and at times rebellious, tending to ignore instructions and drive his own race. Castolletti, however, was a team man and his death in 1957 was certainly a blow to Ferrari as he was equally at home whether driving a racing or a sports-racing car.

One Italian who never really received the praise he deserved was Lorenzo Bandini. He came on the scene when Ferrari had such stars as Phil Hill, John Surtees and Chris Amon as number one drivers, but he more than upheld the prancing horse shield from 1962 to 1967 as a sound back-up man and it was unfortunate that, during his time as a member of the Scuderia, Ferrari's fortunes began on a downward trend.

Like Musso, Castolletti and several other young Ferrari drivers, Bandini was killed when driving one of the red cars; and although the detractors of motor racing and Scuderia Ferrari may whisper that their deaths were unnecessary, and that Enzo had been callous in his reaction to the death toll, nothing could be further from the truth. Ferrari knows the risks as do the drivers, and such is his horror and distress at death on the track that, for many years, he has never attended a race meeting.

Although there were several Americans who drove for Ferrari, only two made any significant impact. Phil Hill became a team member late in 1958, after both Musso and Peter Collins had met with their fatal accidents, and he took a Dino 246 F1 into second place at Monza in the Italian GP and into third in the Moroccan GP. It was not until the European GP at Monza in 1960 that he recorded his first victory, but he was placed on many occasions during 1959. For 1961 Ferrari fielded the 156 F1 one model had a 65-degree V and the other 120-degree V engine. The latter type was used by Phil Hill and, although he won only two grands prix he gained sufficient points in the other events counting towards the world championship to win the drivers' title. The Scuderia had a bad time in 1962 and Enzo and Phil Hill decided it was time to part; Enzo accused Hill of not trying, while Hill complained of the poor handling of the machines.

Even though Richie Ginther, the other American, drove for only two seasons his contribution to the better handling of racing cars should not be forgotten, for he was not only an engineer but also a specialist in aircraft design and used his knowledge when testing the cars. After much experimentation he found that the fitting of spoilers at the front and rear of the cars gave greater stability and better handling, and his pioneer work was to make a significant contribution to the evolution of the racing car.

Ferrari regrouped his resources for 1963 and invited ex-world 500 cc motorcycle champion John Surtees to drive for the Scuderia. During the season Surtees won three important events with the revamped 120-degree V 156 F1 car. By 1964 the 158 F1 was ready; he drove the car throughout the season and scored three major wins, and with a number of second and third places took the drivers' world championship. The year 1965 was mediocre and in 1966 Surtees left Ferrari in mid-season. It was also the year in which the 312 flat-12 boxer unit was introduced, but even drivers of the calibre of Chris Amon and Jacky Ickx could not make any impression on the opposition and had to be content with minor placings. However, the picture changed in 1970 when Ferraris were triumphant in four of the last five grands prix. In the Austrian and Mexican races Ickx and Clay Regazzoni scored a one-two.

Perhaps one of the most brilliant drivers taken on by the works was Niki Lauda. The year was 1974, and great things were expected as he and Regazzoni appeared to make a good team, but it was not until the following year that Lauda won the drivers' title for Ferrari. Lauda had always been a somewhat enigmatic character and it was not long before he and Enzo had their differences which continued over a long period. The break-up occurred at the United States GP at Watkins Glen in 1977 when Lauda walked out, after winning his second world championship. Carlos Reutemann took over in 1978 with Gilles Villeneuve as number two—the latter in his first season showed a certain wildness due to inexperience in Formula 1 racing. However, in 1979 he proved he could also drive with the polished ease of a veteran. Team leader, South African Jody Scheckter, also exhibited a tendency to wildness in his early days of grand prix driving, but as the years passed he has shown a much calmer approach to the sport; by remaining cool but determined he eventually became world drivers' champion in 1979.

Scheckter, driving the highly successful 312 T3 and T4, won three grand prix in the 1979 season: the Belgian, the Monaco and the Italian. His team mate, Gilles Villeneuve, was runner-up in the championship.

In the meantime there is still no sign of an Italian driver capable of sitting behind the wheel of the red cars.

Index

Acknowledgements

The publishers would like to thank the following individuals and organizations for their kind permission to reproduce the photographs in this book, and to Mike Scott of Modena Engineering for his help with providing the car shown on pages 36–37. They would also like to thank the owners who kindly allowed their cars to be photographed and Maranello Concessionaires for their assistance with the latest cars.

Gavin Bain 79; Neil Bruce Photographic 22, 58–59, 78–79 above, 84 inset; L. J. Caddell 36–37, 74–75, 76, 76–77, 83 above; Ian Dawson 14–15, 16–17, 17, 21, 44–45, 46–47, 49 above; Geoffrey Goddard Collection 8–9, 11, 12–13, 20–21, 90, 92; London Art Tech 6–7, 11 inset, 18–19, 27 and inset, 38 below, 38–39 above, 42–43, 43, 62–63, 63 below, 78 above, 88–89, 91 and inset, 93 and insets, 94 inset, 94–95, 95 inset.

All other photographs by Nicky Wright.